AF247627

Arnold Bennett

ALSO BY FRANK SWINNERTON

Rosalind Passes · Nor All Thy Tears · On the Shady Side
The Bright Lights · Sanctuary · Death of a Highbrow
The Woman from Sicily · A Tigress in Prothero
The Grace Divorce · Quadrille · The Sumner Intrigue
A Month in Gordon Square · Master Jim Probity
A Flower for Catherine · The Doctor's Wife Comes to Stay
Faithful Company · English Maiden · A Woman in Sunshine
Thankless Child · The Fortunate Lady · The Two Wives
Harvest Comedy · Elizabeth · The Georgian House
Sketch of a Sinner · A Brood of Ducklings · Summer Storm
The Elder Sister · Young Felix · The Three Lovers · Coquette
September · Shops and Houses · Nocturne · The Chaste Wife
On the Staircase · The Happy Family · The Casement
The Young Idea · The Merry Heart · Some Achieve Greatness

Reflections from a Village · Figures in the Foreground
Background With Chorus · Swinnerton: An Autobiography
The Bookman's London · Londoner's Post · A Galaxy of Fathers
Authors and the Book Trade · The Georgian Literary Scene
Tokefield Papers · A London Bookman
George Gissing: A Critical Study
R. L. Stevenson: A Critical Study
The Reviewing and Criticism of Books (J. M. Dent Memorial
Lecture) · The Cats and Rosemary: A Book for Children

ARNOLD BENNETT

A Last Word

Frank Swinnerton

DOUBLEDAY & COMPANY, INC.
GARDEN CITY, NEW YORK
1978

ISBN: 0-385-14545-4
Library of Congress Catalog Card Number 78-8204

PRINTED IN THE UNITED STATES OF AMERICA
FIRST EDITION IN THE UNITED STATES OF AMERICA

To

Arnold Bennett's

daughter, Virginia

NOTE

I ought to have written this book long ago, when the events it describes were fresh in memory; but as I am a professional writer and amateur gardener with many preoccupations such work has been impossible. Nor, during the lifetime of two of its characters, was I free to speak as plainly as I intend to do. I can assure the reader, however, that everything in the book is drawn either from my own knowledge or from the express report of actual witnesses. Nothing is falsified.

F.S.

ILLUSTRATIONS

Arnold Bennett

1

Arnold Bennett was the eldest of seven children. The sister whom he loved best was named Tertia, and his younger brother, who died after a long illness in 1926, was Sep, or Septimus. Arnold therefore developed early in life a sense of protective responsibility for half-a-dozen juniors. He looked after their welfare, insisted upon giving them fraternal, almost paternal, but never patronizing advice, sent them money (Frank, the solicitor brother, was once rescued from imminent personal disaster), paid the expenses involved in Sep's illness, and paid for the education of Frank's son Richard at Oundle School and Cambridge University. He added to this financial help an avuncular care, writing the boy regular letters which have appeared in print and in quantity.

It was Bennett who cajoled the almost morbidly modest Pauline Smith to continue writing short stories and a novel which are the best pictures extant of life in South Africa. It was Bennett who constituted himself what he called my 'Father in God', and who encouraged such younger men as Siegfried Sassoon, Robert Nichols, and Aldous Huxley. Whenever he heard of a writer suffering hardship he would say 'he has to be *helped*', and he once gave Sassoon a large sum of money for distribution among needy young poets. Once, when I showed him an appeal to myself from Thomas Burke on behalf of a decayed novelist, he asked at once 'What shall you send?' and although he had never met either Burke or his friend he said, when he heard that I had thought of five pounds, 'I should like to do the same'. Out came a loose cheque, carried for just such an emergency; and it was straightway written and handed to me across the table. The recipient of both cheques wrote 'I feel like a dog with *two* tails, both wagging'.

This action of Bennett's was characteristic. It was alleged

by the unkind that he cared only for getting rich; but he had no interest in acquiring wealth. When I grumbled to him that my wife and I had been 'skied' at Covent Garden, he inquired how much I had paid for the tickets; and on my telling him he commented 'that wasn't enough'. I replied that I had not been able to bring myself to pay more; and he cried: 'Don't I know! Once poor, always poor. Sometimes I can't bring myself to take a taxi!'

This reminds me of days long ago, when suburban families in deep poverty drew heavy lace curtains across their downstairs front windows to prevent those walking by from seeing the absence of furniture within. Those were the days of the 'moonlight flit', when many who no longer had any hope of paying their arrears of rent took advantage of the darkness to remove their few sticks and go elsewhere to live. We hear nothing about such people nowadays, when soup kitchens for slum-dwellers make livelier material for sociologists; but in the last years of the nineteenth century they were a feature of urban life.

Bennett belonged to the clan of the gentle (not 'genteel') poor. So, in childhood, did I. Children brought up in more protected circumstances cannot realize how such self-respecting poverty, where pride dictates concealment of need, can affect the outlook of those less fortunate. These latter resolve that when they grow up they will never fall again to such humiliation.

In the same way poor children, who would now be described as 'deprived' or 'underprivileged', were incapable of the boast, so often made by intellectual snobs of the Twenties, that they cared only for the First Class in literature and art. They begin to write, as Bennett did, and as many other journalists do, with modest ambitions, hoping thereby to turn irresistible inclination to some as yet undetermined account. The impulse to write is there; a living has to be earned; impulse and need are compatible; hacks are made by the thousand. May I be allowed to remark that it is possible to be both hack and snob?

Bennett himself, rejoicing as a boy in the works of Eugène Sue and Ouida, at first had no expectation of being able to do better than they. He wrote some paragraphs for a local newspaper; those were the beginnings of his voluminous journalism.

But he also longed for romance, which is the reason why he ventured into that field with such tales as *The Grand Babylon Hotel* and *The Gates of Wrath*. He saw himself, not as a 'first class' writer, impressing superior minds, but as a journeyman capable of writing articles on 'How a Case is prepared for trial' and serial novelettes which could be sold outright to a Newspaper Syndicate for seventy-five pounds apiece.

Bennett came to London when young as a solicitors' clerk, and by a lucky chance lodged in a Chelsea house where several juvenile artists were also living. He for the first time heard things described by his colleagues as 'beautiful', an adjective never used in his provincial surroundings. 'I perceived', he wrote years later, 'that I must begin life again!'

His critical faculty developed. He became a bibliophile. He found that his Chelsea friends expected him to become an original writer of quality. As reported in that remarkable piece of autobiography, *The Truth about an Author*, he one day exclaimed 'By Heaven! I will write a novel!'

The novel was *A Man from the North*, which has recently been reprinted with success by Hamish Hamilton eighty years after its first publication; but first he had written a short story called *A Letter Home*. This was rejected by the Editor of *Tit-bits* as below the paper's literary standard, but was printed in *The Yellow Book*. The praise given to this story, and John Lane's acceptance of *A Man from the North* (Lane's 'reader' being John Buchan), aroused Bennett's self-esteem. He still regarded himself as a composer of serial stories, and as a journalist with the 'policy of never declining work that I am practically challenged to do'; but reading of the great French and Russian novelists had stirred a more profound ambition. He decided to go to Paris, where great novelists in the realistic tradition were still living and working.

I think he may have been led to take this step by learning that George Moore, for whose realistic works of fiction he had developed an admiration, had spent several formative years in the French capital. The admiration lasted, and Moore subsequently professed equal admiration for one whom he regarded as a disciple. At any rate Bennett, once in Paris, learned to speak and write French idiomatically, to the amusement of Wells, who made fun of his use of French phrases. Nevertheless, Bennett kept his English, and caused equal amusement to French colleagues by violently describing some inferior book as 'putride'. Bennett did not object to ridicule of himself; though not courting it, he never 'rose' to it as a more conceited man would have done. He was in France to learn.

It was his habit to take his meals at the popular restaurants known by the name of their proprietor, which was Duval; and one day when he was sitting at his usual table in one of those establishments he witnessed a scene which was to change the course of his life. A fussy old woman entered, dropped her baggage, could not settle on a table which would suit her, and flitted here and there, causing a commotion, and making everybody in the restaurant, including a beautiful waitress of whom Bennett had expected more humanity, laugh with contemptuous ridicule of an eccentric.

Bennett alone did not laugh. Being fundamentally romantic, he thought to himself: 'This old woman is considered crazy. But she must once have been young, perhaps lovely'. Almost instantly, he perceived the tragedy of age; and in considering this tragedy he resolved to write a novel of which inexorable Time should be the theme. Other work had to be done, including one of the best of his minor novels, *Whom God hath Joined*; but he gave much thought in the next few months to what he now called *The Two Old Women*, and what was ultimately *The Old Wives' Tale*.

The one old woman in the restaurant had become two, in accordance with a well-established convention of British fiction and drama. Two sisters can be used for both intimacy and contrast, as was shown by Walter Scott in *The Heart of Midlothian* and by Jane Austen in *Pride and Prejudice* and *Sense and Sensibility*. And since Bennett's knowledge of character and manners had been derived from experience of lower middle class life in the Potteries, he determined to make his sisters natives of that District. *The Old Wives' Tale* was positively begun in October, 1907, and was finished in August, 1908.

It was written largely in Paris, where Bennett frequented the company of professional writers and artists, and matured his understanding of the subtleties of aesthetic criticism. In Paris, also, he made the acquaintance of another young novelist and dramatist, William Somerset Maugham, a young painter, Gerald Kelly, who said he believed himself to be the model for all Maugham's sketches of bad artists, Berta Ruck, who wrote novelettes and became the wife of Oliver Onions, and, among many others, a young woman from the French provinces, Marguerite Soulié.

Marguerite Soulié became his mistress; and when he was taken dangerously ill with typhoid fever she nursed him with such unselfish devotion that he made an almost miraculous recovery. He was medically advised to leave Paris for a period of convalescence; and Marguerite went to see him safely aboard a train bound, I think, for the Riviera.

They were about to part when Bennett said in his abrupt way: 'Do you know what my friends are telling me? They are saying I ought to marry you'. Marguerite's response (I cannot guarantee the exact words; but my informant was Bennett himself) was: 'Oh, don't dazzle me with such a prospect if you are not serious!' Convinced that he was in earnest, she was that day, and for long afterwards, a happy woman.

Once married, they went to live in Fontainebleau, where they were visited by, among others, George Doran, who eventually published *The Old Wives' Tale* in the United States with such energy that he made it the talk of the country. A visit from Bennett to America produced a welcome comparable only to that given to Charles Dickens seventy years earlier. When I was there more than a dozen years afterwards the only adverse memory of him was that when served with Terrapin at a banquet in his honour he asked 'What is this, I say?' and, on being told, added, regardful of his delicate digestion, 'Then I shall not eat it'.

After such international success it was inevitable that legends should spread about a man who had come, unknown, from the Potteries and who had a number of instinctive traits. For one thing, he had a North Country accent. For another, he wrote books of very different orders and unequal quality; and when one of his books dealt relishingly with the adventures of a 'card' or cheeky careerist, it was assumed that this artful character was a self-portrait, whereas it was the highly inventive study of a schoolmate named Hales. In an early popular serial story he humorously described a luxury hotel: therefore he was pictured as a gaping lad who was infatuated with the grandiose. The lights of London had beckoned; and he had come to town to make a fortune.

The truth was that even after success he stayed, well content, at the Strand Palace Hotel, which in spite of its name, was a comfortable place altogether free from ostentation. It provided him with something which in those days was not a regulation fitting—a bedside light by which he could read during long periods of neuralgic insomnia.

His interest in great hotels arose from curiosity as to their marvellous organization. How did they manage to satisfy the tastes and needs of so many people? How was it that members of the staff worked so well together? What went on behind the scenes? What were the relations between the cooks and the management? Organization was a word constantly on his lips. He 'organized' his own life of twenty-four hours a day, and he loved punctuality and efficiency. Hence, ultimately, the intensive study revealed in *Imperial Palace*, which, he always insisted, was *not* the Savoy.

A further legend was derived from the facts that when *The Old Wives' Tale* was published he had reached the age of forty and married a Frenchwoman. So the story was invented that in youth he had deliberately planned to write pot-boilers until he reached that age, when he would marry a Frenchwoman, and produce a masterpiece. This took no account of *A Man from the North*, *Anna of the Five Towns*, and *Whom God hath Joined*, which certainly were not pot-boilers; and of course no account of something that only his friends know about, the abortive love affair with a heartless American girl in Paris. Nevertheless the legend persists and forms the basis of most adverse judgment upon a man who combined fun and seriousness with a total lack of self-importance.

The final legend was that his mind was dominated by a love of money. Much was made of the fact that he was said to have left, at death, the large sum of thirty thousand pounds. What was not understood was that this sum represented an official valuation of his copyrights. In fact I believe he left only a few thousand pounds; and I know that his executor, Alistair Tayler, paid the Death Duties out of his own pocket.

As to his attitude to work and personal affairs, he noted in 1905 that Eden Phillpotts and H. G. Wells were more interested in money that he was, and he wrote in an early page of the *Journal* before he was thirty years of age and before the publication of his first book:

'An artist works only to satisfy himself, and for the applause and appreciation neither of his fellows alive nor his fellows yet unborn. I would not care a bilberry for posterity. I should be my own justest judge from whom there would be no appeal; and having satisfied him (whether he was right or wrong) I should be content—as an artist. As a *man*, I should be disgusted if I could not earn plenty of money and the praise of the discriminating.'

2

As this book is to be a portrait of Arnold Bennett as he was known to his friends, it may be thought that I should say nothing about myself. On the other hand curiosity has been expressed regarding my apparent jump from suburban obscurity into familiar association with two or three celebrated seniors. I shall therefore ask the reader's pardon for introducing this subject.

Being employed, in the early years of the century, from 1901 until 1907, as an assistant in the publishing firm of J. M. Dent & Co, who were celebrated for their pocket editions, the Temple Shakespeare and the Temple Classics, as they were later to be for Everyman's Library, I saw all the weekly journals specializing in political commentary and reviews of new books.

There was *The Athenaeum*, a very grave production, whose reviewers, including Swinburne's friend Theodore Watts-Dunton, were haughtily severe towards pretentious or scamped literary production. Its editor was Vernon Rendall, who as a very old man became an intimate correspondent and friend. There was *The Saturday Review*, living up to a reputation for iconoclasm (Bernard Shaw was still its dramatic critic, dealing trenchantly with melodrama and the 'well-made' play). And there was the rather prudish *Spectator* under St Loe Strachey's editorship, which found the last scene in one of Henry Seton Merriman's novels 'prurient', but which was probably better than it seemed to such young scanners as myself.

The two weeklies I liked best were *The Speaker* and *The Academy*. The former was Liberal in politics, and very humane, as one would expect of a paper edited by J. L. Hammond; the latter, edited by a strange character named Lewis Hind, and run as a hobby by a rich pill- and ointment-maker, sported a grey cover bearing a Beggarstaff outline drawing and was printed upon cream paper. Its contributors, although I did not know it, included Lionel Johnson, E. V. Lucas, and Wilfred Whitten, the founder of *John o' London's Weekly*. How strange it seems, in retrospect, to think that, many years later, I should have been asked to take the job of writing Whitten's regular 'Letter to Gog and Magog' in that paper!

I must have read the critical weeklies without much comprehension from the age of sixteen; but by the time I was eighteen I had been lent or given to Dent's Irish manager, W. G. Stirret, various French and Russian novels in English translations, and had begun to experiment in the writing of novels of my own. Therefore one explanation of a preference for *The Speaker* and *The Academy* may have been that in *The Speaker* Edward Garnett, who said that 'the most serious and significant of all literary forms in the modern world is the novel', was devoting many columns to the establishment of that proposition, while in *The Academy* appeared articles on such subjects as 'English and French Fiction in the Nineteenth Century' and 'The Fallow Fields of Fiction'.

I am sure of those things because I cut out the articles and pasted them into several albums which are still, yellowed and broken-backed, in existence. Garnett was an enthusiast for the exquisite art of Turgenev, whom I already, thanks to Stirret, admired very much; the articles in *The Academy* were signed with initials only. I had not the prescience to guess that the initials 'E.A.B.' stood for the full names of Enoch Arnold Bennett.

There also appeared serially in *The Academy* an extremely amusing anonymous work called 'The Truth about an Author'. I cut out the instalments and preserved them until I was able to buy, for sixpence, a 'remaindered' copy of the still anonymous complete book. The Author took advantage of his anonymity to laugh and boast his way through early adventures in journalism and what has since been called, very contemptuously, pot-boiling. What he related was true; but his manner suggested that, besides being cocky, he was a *blagueur*.

Later on, my bookish friends and I were delighted with certain literary causeries appearing in another weekly, *The New Age*. This was a brilliant paper, in which Shaw, Belloc, Gilbert Chesterton, and others argued sportively together; and it is one of my happy memories that the editor, A. R. Orage, accepted an article of mine entitled 'Modern Realism', and actually paid for it with a postal order for ten shillings. I was then in my very early twenties. This article, I afterwards found, had been cut out and preserved by Bennett.

At the beginning of 1909 I published my first novel, *The Merry Heart.* Though scathingly condemned by my friends, one of whom, before he had read a word of it, remarked 'of course I don't know how bad a book may be and yet get published', this book was lucky enough to receive praise from generous strangers in the Press, including Basil de Sélincourt in *The Manchester Guardian*; while *The Academy* told its readers that *The Merry Heart* 'reproduced, with an accuracy little less than amazing, the manners and habits of speech of lower middle-class society'.

My friends were astonished, delighted, and unconvinced by those reviews. Only a fellow-clerk, who had enjoyed the book, said: 'Have you read any of Arnold Bennett's novels? I think you'd like them. You and he have the same kind of humour.'

I read *A Great Man*; and went on to *The Grand Babylon Hotel*, *The Old Wives' Tale*, and *Clayhanger*. This was in the years 1909 and 1910, when I was between the ages of 24 and 25; and having laughed at *A Great Man* I formed a notable admiration for the author of *The Old Wives' Tale* and *Clayhanger*. I had no expectation of acquaintance with him, and indeed thought myself merely an amateur who wrote for his own amusement; but the reviews of *The Merry Heart* had been encouraging, and when my second novel, *The Young Idea*, was published immediately after my 26th birthday, I determined to express my admiration by sending Bennett a copy of it.

I had never done anything of this kind before, and I desired him not to acknowledge the gift. According to my recollection, I wrote: 'Having read several of your novels, I think you ought to read one of mine.' This approach, I now believe, probably amused Bennett very much; and as Swinnerton is a Staffordshire name (there is even a village called Swinnerton in the neighbourhood of Stone) it may have quickened his interest in the book. A postcard of acknowledgment preceded a very long and extraordinary letter. I quote some of this letter here, not in vainglory, but to show Bennett's scrupulousness and generosity to an unknown:

'Dear Mr Frank Swinnterton, I have read *The Young Idea*. I am sorry *The New Age* has already reviewed it (I did not see the review) as otherwise I should have discussed it myself in *The New Age*. . . . Nobody who has a genuine taste for literature and who has really read your book could possibly fail to admire it, and deeply to respect you as an artist. But the trouble will be to get reviewers really to read it. I had some difficulty at first in yielding myself to it, and I am sure that vast numbers of professional journalistic reviewers would be capable of going through it without perceiving its extraordinary qualities. The fact is I read about 100 pages myself before I properly grasped your method, and the extreme fineness and originality of it.

'You resemble Henry James more nearly than any other writer I know. I do not mean this particularly for a compliment. I merely state the fact. In my opinion the book is very good indeed. . . . It is written throughout with the most exquisite justesse. I don't mean justice. . . . But what struck me occasionally was that you restrained your emotion somewhat, and were afraid to give rein to your emotion. I know by my own experience that one of the last things learnt by a writer who tries to be realistic is to let himself go a bit lyrically in the larger crises. The fact is, he is afraid of his own criticism. . . .

'I have not said anything about a lot of fine qualities that I perceive in *The Young Idea*. But they are in my mind. The book is profound.

'Believe me, Cordially yours, Arnold Bennett.'

This remarkable letter was followed shortly afterwards by an invitation to lunch at the Authors' Club, then housed in a block of flats near Westminster known as Whitehall Court. Our meeting began badly, for another guest, Alice Perrin, a novelist of Indian life, arrived simultaneously with myself. There was what seemed to be an altercation between my host and this lady, who had mistaken the date of their appointment and come a week too early. Mrs Perrin assured Bennett that she could easily lunch elsewhere, and she left; but both he and I were greatly embarrassed by the scene.

When we were alone, I said 'I could have come another day'. His reply was 'Not at all. She's wrong. She was asked for next week, to meet my wife, who's away'. But his face had reddened; and we were both silent, deeply troubled by what we knew must have been a humiliation for Mrs Perrin. It took some time for our disturbed feelings to quieten.

The man I now followed to our table in the Club was in his early forties, clear-complexioned, with the much-publicized and much-caricatured quiff of hair and a rigid-shouldered walk in which he seemed forced to move slightly to one side at every step. One fact I noticed was that his eyes, although healthy and direct in gaze, and of a warm brown, looked tired because the lid of one of them was heavy. The forehead was square, and his aspect extraordinarily benign. Somerset Maugham once said in print that Bennett had an aura of benevolence; to which I would add that nobody, meeting him, could doubt his honesty. Candour might be enriched by kindness, or humour; but evasiveness, as it is frequently practised by more sophisticated men, was impossible to him.

He was perhaps an inch taller than myself, five feet ten inches; an abruptness of speech was explained by the fact that he stammered badly. The stammer was not, like Maugham's, an occasional 'm-m-m', but was a total inability to utter any word at all. He would say 'and er . . . and er . . . and er . . .'; his jaw trembled; he persisted, ignoring any well-meant or officious help and the escape of any evasive substitution, until he managed to complete the sentence he had begun. This struggle was truly painful to witness and to share.

Now the stammer was made worse by recent embarrassment, so that I found it hard to understand what he was determined to say. Another difficulty was his voice, which I once wrongly described as shrill. It had not the curious nasal high pitch of Wells's, with its delightful little pips of mischievious laughter. Nor did it resemble the Strachean bleat and ascent to falsetto (which I suspected of being an affectation). Rather, it was a rough creak, shrill only by comparison with the resonance of A. G. Gardiner or the easy flow of Compton Mackenzie's baritone. Gardiner was a fine public speaker, clearly audible at the back of a large hall; Mackenzie, with acting in his blood, commanded every vocal *nuance*. In Bennett's case the rasp and abruptness suggested a defective larynx.

Another ghastly moment came when, owing to his habit of

using the pronoun 'he' instead of naming the person he was speaking about, we suddenly found that he had been extolling Thomas Hardy, while I had assumed our subject to be George Meredith. I thought 'Oh golly! This is going to be dreadful!'

We got on better when he asked if I had read Herbert Spencer's *Study of Sociology.* I had done so. He beamed, and, using the flat 'a' of the Northcountryman, exclaimed 'It's like a *bath*!' Something equally fortunate occurred when he caught sight of a man at a neighbouring table. Jerking his head, and lowering his voice, he said 'Over there . . . is the most successful novelist in England!' I whispered, in awe, 'Not *Charles Garvice*?' I was right; and Bennett told the man's story.

It was that Garvice, a hack, having written many novelettes for a girls' paper, selling them outright, discovered that the paper was in the market as a property. In some way, not disclosed, he had arranged to buy the paper, thereby recovering all rights in his novelettes. He then proceeded to publish the tales as sixpenny paper-bound books. They sold in many thousands; and Garvice became rich 'beyond the dreams of avarice'.

We turned to my own novel, of which the sales had been about six hundred copies; and I made another *gaffe*. Bennett praised it so highly that I had qualms. I said 'Are you sure you're not making a mistake about me?' This was a deadly affront to a man absolutely sure of his own judgment. He almost shouted '*I'm* making no mistake! Don't you believe in yourself?' When I said 'Not to that extent', he eyed me ferociously. I do not remember his verbal retort.

Once more we passed to greater ease. He showed me the manuscript of *Hilda Lessways*, which he was then writing; and mentioned that in spite of its fame *The Old Wives' Tale* had sold fewer than six thousand in England. As I left, on finding that although, as an anonymous reception clerk at Dent's, I had spoken to a number of famous people, I had no personal acquaintance with any of them, he asked if I would like to meet his friend H. G. Wells. At my sparkle of pleasure, he made a gloomy and most significant declaration. It was 'He *talks*, you know. I can't do that.'

3

Three years passed, during which I received a number of long and encouraging letters, all written in his extremely small, beautiful hand. We did not meet, however, as he was still in France; and my first encounter with H. G. Wells came about through no action of his. In the year 1912 I published two books, the first of them a novel called *The Happy Family*, and the second a critical study of George Gissing, whom he had not known. I do not remember whether he commented upon the latter.

When it was published, I received a letter from John Middleton Murry, who was editing what would now be called an *avant garde* periodical called *Rhythm*. Murry announced that Wells had written for *Rhythm* an enthusiastic review of my book on Gissing, and he asked me to tea in a flat in Chancery Lane, where he lived with his wife, Katherine Mansfield. By coincidence, Katherine Mansfield proved to have been the writer of a cordial review in *The Westminster Gazette* of my novel, published three months earlier; so that I entered this ambitious little circle under good auspices.

I need not speak further of the association which followed; but must mention that Wells invited me to Sunday supper in his Hampstead home, where the other guests were Henry Arthur Jones, the dramatist, William Rothenstein, the artist, and H. C. Marillier, who ran the business inaugurated by William Morris. This was the beginning of another friendship.

My study of Gissing's tragic character led me to invent a young man for my next novel, *On the Staircase*, who had some of Gissing's traits; and it was this book, published in the Spring of 1914, which led Arnold Bennett to ask me to lunch for the second time. He was in England; and he wrote 'there is something in the book that makes me want to see you again'.

No indication was given of what the 'something' was; but I was invited to lunch at the Berkeley Hotel to meet Mrs Bennett.

This, then, was my first encounter with Marguerite. Tall, dark, and gracious to a young English novelist of whom her husband spoke highly, she said little; and what little she said was often in French. I was much more at ease that day than I had been at the Authors' Club, perhaps because Marguerite was present, but more probably because, in the interval, I had gained social experience and formed friendships with several young novelists of my own age, including Gilbert Cannan, Compton Mackenzie, and Hugh Walpole. Bennett, too, had cast off shyness. Moreover, as a stammerer, he was able to relax in the company of one who has never been known to stammer.

In the course of luncheon he suddenly demanded 'Have you done *much* yachting, I say?' I, astonished, replied 'I've never been on a yacht in my life'. Bennett cried 'But that . . . But that . . . about the bell buoy! In your book!'

It took me a moment to understand what he meant. I had forgotten all about a passage in *On the Staircase* which described how the Gissing-like hero, half-poet, half-dreamer, moved to despair by recognition of his loneliness in an uncaring world, and sitting alone in his bed-sitter, had been visited by the landlady's pretty, ignorant daughter, Cissie. Her nearness in such circumstances, and his need of love, affected him so much that he could not resist the impulse to clutch her hand. The girl, equally moved, came closer.

The narrative continued:

> ' "Oh, what is it, what is it?" she said, half-crying. He felt her hand wrenched free, and her arms about him, and his face was held tightly against her soft breast. For an eternity they seemed to stay so, until Cissie slipped to her knees. Now Velancourt's arms were around her shoulders, and her face was fiercely against his.
>
> ' "Kiss me. Kiss me!" she begged.
>
> ' "Oh, my dear!" He felt warm kisses upon his own lips, hurried, eager.
>
> ' "Dear, let me go . . . Let me go. They'll notice. I . . . let me go".

'He let her go, and she pressed back into his arms. He was terribly excited; but not happy. Something kept saying in his head: "It's done, it's done, it's done," over and over again, like a curfew or the dreadful ringing of a buoy at night in a dark sea.'

'Have you done *much* yachting, I say?'

At last I understood.

'Oh, I just thought it would be a very frightening sound'.

He pondered my reply. Since he was a realist, who used his close observation, and even his own character, as a basis for all his 'serious' fiction, as can be seen in *These Twain* and *Lord Raingo*, in which his relations with, respectively, Marguerite and Dorothy Cheston are detailed, he assumed that I, as another realist, must do the same. I, on the contrary, am by no means observant, but rely upon intuition for many incidents apparently real. The result of his pondering produced another stammered exclamation.

'You . . . you . . . must come on the yacht'.

He meant his own yacht; but as was afterwards pointed out to me by a French friend of both Bennetts, the Abbé Dimnet, he always used the impersonal word. It was 'the yacht', or 'the house', while Marguerite said 'my 'ouse' or 'my garden'. In both cases the custom was natural.

This was in the Spring of 1914. By then Bennett had decided to return to England to live. He gave up his home in Fontainebleau, and bought one at Thorpe-le-Soken, near the Essex coast and within easy reach of a harbour where a boat could be moored. Increased income from books, plays, and unceasing journalism enabled him to indulge a love of the sea—I was told by his brother-in-law, William Kennerley, that he was a very strong swimmer; and it had been a dream from boyhood that he might own a yacht.

Marguerite, unfortunately, was nothing of a sailor. Therefore he was in need of male companionship for short voyages across the English Channel, into the North Sea, and to the Mediterranean coastal resorts. Hence his leap to the conclusion that I must once have heard a bell at night in a dark sea, and his wish to meet me again.

Four months later, at the end of July, 1914, on returning from the Leipsic Book Fair, where my employers had an exhibit, I found waiting an invitation to spend a weekend on *Velsa*. These were days immediately before the opening of the First World War. Although I had been in Berlin at the time the Austrian Crown Prince was assassinated, neither Bennett nor I dreamed of what was to follow.

I joined *Velsa*, which had both sails and a motor, with captain, a cook, and a single deck hand, at Westminster Bridge; and we set off with great dignity down the Thames. We dined; I was rowed by my host in pitch darkness and a state of concealed terror across the harbour at Holehaven; and we had a greal deal of literary conversation. Next morning, thanks to Winston Churchill's timely mobilization of the Fleet, we found ourselves passing close to a splendid assembly of gigantic cruisers, each of which, of course, flew the White Ensign.

Bennett, as a member of the Royal Thames Yacht Club, was entitled to use the Blue Ensign, and therefore to receive a salute from every one of His Majesty's ships of war. To my great, but hidden, amusement our captain stood running his little flag up and down, while a stir on each of the cruisers was followed by the dipping and hoisting of the White Ensign. Bennett was not amused. He stood erect, watching the performance with deep satisfaction. Afterwards, he expressed resentment at the fact that when, earlier in the year, *Velsa* had sailed into Kiel Harbour no notice had been taken of her.

This was the beginning of the richest of all my happy friendships with men and women of every kind. In spite of the seventeen years' difference in our ages it was to last, unblemished, until Bennett's death in 1931.

4

It so happened that I was very ill in the Autumn of 1914, losing great quantities of blood and albumen, and very nearly dying. Altogether I was out of action for six months. When well again, I found that neither Wells nor Bennett had forgotten me. They seem to have decided, independently, that I needed 'looking after'. It is so long ago, that I have forgotten the details; but I was constantly invited to spend weekends in their homes in the country, with Wells at Easton, with Bennett at Thorpe-le-Soken. Since I am writing about Bennett, and not Wells, I shall speak exclusively of visits to the former.

There I met, besides members of the Bennett family, older friends who have become nameless in memory; but I recall E. A. Rickards, the architect; Pauline Smith, the South African author of *The Little Karoo* (who eventually wrote a gratefully affectionate tribute to her kind and insistent mentor); a doctor named Shufflebotham, whom Bennett always called 'Shuf'; and Maurice Marston, organizer of the National Book Council.

Here, too, I first made the acquaintance of Winifred Nerney, Bennett's magnificent secretary. This book owes much to Winifred, who not only told me many things which could only have been known to a young woman of insight closely domesticated with the Bennetts, but gave me a mass of letters and other papers of vital interest. I shall speak of her later, for we were friends to the end of her life and she was one of the most candid persons I ever met.

Finally, there were seven or eight professional soldiers, who, being stationed in the district, were constantly in the house. It was one of these soldiers who, because of a ridiculous story I told, christened me 'Henry', a name by which Bennett addressed me ever afterwards.

French Empire furniture seemed to predominate in the living rooms at Comarques; it was the first over-heated house I had met with; and it had a large garden, with greenhouses—also a novelty to me. There were two dogs, one a yapping pet of Marguerite's named Fifi, the other an artful dachshund, Rex, who was constantly scheming to go on walks by himself. A Ford car of the kind known as a 'flivver' was driven with great seriousness by Bennett and often, in cold weather, took strong men a long time to start.

It was in this car that we sometimes drove to Frinton-on-Sea, and it was in Frinton that I had the unique experience of seeing an elderly lady drink cocktails through her black lace veil for the sake of continuing satisfaction. And there lived in the neighbourhood an affable spinster who figures in *The Price of Love* as 'Sensible Winnie, but apt to skid'. This lady had the keenest nose for innuendo that I have ever noticed, and her laugh still crackles in my ears.

Sometimes the soldiers came on horseback, bringing a mount for Bennett, who rode it with immense dignity but at no great pace. Sometimes there were games of lawn tennis, which he played from the baseline in his shirtsleeves and displaying brilliant red or patterned braces. He never moved much; but he was an efficient player.

The atmosphere of Comarques was normally calm; but the calm was sometimes broken by what would nowadays be called 'confrontations' in which Bennett's obstinate refusal to be ruffled was at variance with Marguerite's explosive vehemence. There is no doubt in my mind that the character of Hilda Lessways, who in *Clayhanger* was enigmatic, changed in *These Twain* into something very like Marguerite. The conflict between Edwin and Hilda in the latter book could well have been an echo of scenes at Comarques.

Marguerite, before an accepted friend, as I became, did what many wives do in comparable circumstances. She deliberately introduced her complaints into mealtime conversation, rallying Arnold jocosely (she had no real humour) about some personal divergence, and, losing her temper at his resolute unresponsiveness, beginning to storm. If her assertions became too wild, Bennett would sometimes remark 'That . . . is not true, Marguerite', which made her furious. He did not comment upon such outbreaks; and I appreciated the fact that, as

Vittoria Sanna pointed out in her study, *Arnold Bennett e i Romanza delle Cinque Citta*, he had absorbed the stoic teachings of Marcus Aurelius and Epictetus. Marguerite was unquainted with these Masters.

That being so, she was really happiest when the professional soldiers, whom she always called 'de offissair', viewed her with admiration. It was gratifying to be considered, as she was, physically, 'a very fine woman'. A Stoic, whatever his inner emotion, cannot yield himself to passion. I thought, and still think, that instinctive self-control inhibited any show of amorousness in Bennett.

Marguerite, when playful, would sometimes tease him by using his first name, Enoch, to which he replied with the exclamation 'Hell!' She told me that his mother, if he was ever sportively nonsensical, always quelled him, as she had done in childhood, with the stern rebuke 'Nay, Enoch!' The name recalled days of repression, when his duty was pointed out and insisted upon. It took him back instantly to Hanley, where the weight of responsibility for his juniors was a heavy burden. It also revealed the fact that his mother was unimpressed by either his gifts or his fame.

There were not many such sallies. I was told by Winifred Nerney that Marguerite was a sly woman, over suspicious and inquisitive. She would, it appears, ransack the drawers of his desk and read the little notebooks in which he recorded ideas for stories or articles, in case they held the names and addresses of other women. Once, to her fury, she forced the lock of a drawer containing many long letters from herself, only to find that a number of them had not been opened. These unopened letters are now in my possession, still unopened.

I did not consider her at all sly. She was an egoist who felt very much alone in England, among people who in those days took pride in concealing all excitement; and she was under great strain as a result of the terrible devastation of her own country.

That was one point. Another was her childlessness, which she never mentioned to myself, but which she enlarged upon to one of his sisters, Mrs Beardmore, and to a fellow Frenchwoman, Mrs Belloc Lowndes. Mrs Beardmore, a stern J.P. of magistral carriage, spoke of the matter to a journalist who printed her views. Mrs Belloc Lowndes referred to the matter in print. But I do not know the truth. What seems to me more important is the intense pride she felt in his reputation and his earnings, which latter she may have ascertained by some of her explorations. The pride was amusingly shown in 1919, when a novel of mine called *September*, dedicated to herself, sold five thousand copies in England and seventeen thousand in America. On my next arrival at Comarques she greeted me with the demand 'Well, Frank, 'ow do you like being a success?' I replied 'It's very pleasant', and her almost sneering reply was 'Hein! But you are not yet Arnold Bennett!' She meant no harm. It was simply an expression of her pride in him. This did not prevent her from saying on another occasion '*I* am de artiss in dis family!'

I was early given an illustration of Marguerite's inquisitiveness and Arnold's naive and, as it proved, useless determination to frustrate it. He had a secret craze for buying pictures. Marguerite did not approve the craze. In telling me this, one day, he confessed that he often bought a picture and hid it under his bed for several weeks. Later, he hung it up. When challenged by Marguerite with having acquired something new and expensive, he would say, carelessly 'That? Oh, I've had it . . . for a long time'. But Marguerite, within a day or two of his confession to me, murmured in my ear 'I know what he do. He buy a picture, hide it, and I find it. I say "Oh, Arnole, I see you 'ave a new picture", and he say "Oh, I 'have 'ad that a long time". But I know!' Evidently she was in the habit of looking under beds as well as into locked drawers!

He never accused her of prying. He never complained about her at all. His professed attitude to women was that they were mysterious and incalculable children who had to be, not 'helped', but humoured.

Other aspects of the *ménage* struck me. One was Bennett's insistence that everything should be orderly. He would go through newspapers which visitors had rumpled and thrown aside, folding them carefully into their original neatness. He would acknowledge little services done him by his niece or his nephew with the words 'Thank me'. He went for long solitary walks along the lanes near Comarques to 'get ideas' for his day's work; and one of his favourite words was 'organized'. My own methods of work were not, he said, 'properly organized'. This led him to accuse me of being temperamentally 'idle', which I am. But he did this, as he did everything, humorously; and I had one quality which atoned in his eyes for much that was sinful—a habit of being punctual.

Marguerite explained that as he suffered from insomnia it was his custom to get up at half-past five in the morning, brew himself a cup of tea, and work until nine o'clock breakfast. He would then arrive at table well content, boasting that 'I have written five (or sometimes six or seven) hundred words this morning. All . . . of the best'. Then, ever industrious, he would return to his desk, doing more work or writing more letters, some of them long ones, in a tiny script or in shorthand for Winifred Nerney to decipher and type. The number of letters written daily was stupendous. After lunch, he would say 'We-ll, I must have a sleep' and disappear for an hour.

Marguerite did not disappear. She walked about 'my garden' and into the greenhouses, where she cut melons or grapes before they were ready for table, bringing them back to the house in triumph, once indignantly complaining to me that the infuriated gardener looked at her '*comme un assassin*'. She developed social ambitions, and resented—but always as if it were a great joke—the fact that a certain Lady Byng, the *grande dame* of the district, hogged all the limelight.

Marguerite also drove the car, and always managed to return home safely. When Pauline Smith stayed at Comarques, official appeals for petrol economy were disregarded, and Pauline was taken for long journeys about the countryside. After one such excursion, boastfully described to us by Marguerite, Bennett asked Pauline if she also had enjoyed the tour, and, when told that she had done so, said grimly 'I'm surprised'. The implication could not be missed. It filled the gentle Pauline with a sense of guilt. But Marguerite's reaction was violent. She defended herself. She had been accused of betraying 'poor Fwonce' by a waste of petrol.

Poor woman! Bennett was a kind and considerate husband, but not an 'easy' man to live with, especially when his companion was a woman of moods and emotional extravagance. He neither raised his voice nor quarrelled; but his look of grave disapproval on that occasion, as I am sure on many others, was intolerable to one whose need was for constant flattery. Marguerite regarded herself, not only as Marguerite, but as the representative of her nation among critical foreigners; and as the War progressed, and news grew ever more humiliating to her, the cry of 'Poor Fwonce' became louder.

I particularly emphasize this point, as I think her concern with France led to hatred of British reserve, and created mental disturbance which had lasting effects.

As I am on the subject of Bennett's domestic manner, I think it appropriate to mention an episode relating to Winifred Nerney. It is that after being his strictly-drilled secretary for a week she went to her mother, with whom she lived, wrathfully exclaiming 'The happiest day of my life will be the one when I give that man a month's notice!'

The day never came. She stayed loyally and devotedly until the death of a much loved employer nearly twenty years later; and when he died she gave me all the carefully preserved letters and postcards (some of them in shorthand) which he had ever written to her, together with other mementoes of an association full of mutual confidence and respect. She disclaimed the 'efficiency' with which she was credited. 'I'm not really efficient', she wrote; 'but I like work, have a passion for getting things done, and when I worked for A.B. I could do fourteen hours a day for long periods, as when I was typing a novel, because I had a constitution of iron'.

At Christmas-time, 1921, when beset by matrimonial trouble, Bennett wrote to her, with characteristically restrained emotion 'I want to wish you the best wishes, and to thank you very much for the extremely sympathetic and valuable help which you have given to me during recent events. I have greatly appreciated it. I daresay that my manner is often rather curt, but no doubt after all these years you understand that my feelings towards you are not precisely cold'.

5

It was in November, 1917, that Bennett first met Lord Beaverbrook, owner of *The Daily Express*, and *The Evening Standard*. At their second meeting, some days later, the two men went together to an exhibition at the Leicester Gallery; and, having identified an etching which Bennett had praised during lunch, Beaverbrook bought and presented it as a gift. Bennett was a little surprised at the gesture, which he described as 'brusque'; but he was impressed by Beaverbrook's unhesitating power to act like a millionaire. A new friendship was formed; his life thereforward took a new direction.

Hitherto he had been used to the company of professional writers, editors, and artists, all of whom in some degree shared his own humane interests. Now he found himself elected, without consultation, to an exclusive and 'secret' set known to its members as The Other Club, where he met notable men of the Great World. Pride insisted that he should give no outward sign of unfamiliarity with this World. He did not rejoice, as one biographer unkindly suggested, at the thought of being 'in the swim', and he did not desert his old friends; but he was made, willy nilly, a public man, as opposed to a novelist, journalist, and dramatist of repute. He also gathered, still without intention, a number of zealous enemies. It was a new experience.

I have sometimes thought that Beaverbrook was Bennett's Evil Genius; but if an Evil Genius he was at least a genius with a quick eye for competence and weakness in other men and an unconquerable belief in the value of incessant publicity. Bold and ruthless, he was in time of War invaluable to the State. The society he kept ranged from equally bold and ruthless politicians such as Winston Churchill and F. E. Smith, Lord Birkenhead, to the most sophisticated young women of their generation. Bennett was introduced to this society. He was also offered a post in the Ministry of Information, then under Beaverbrook's control, involving responsibility for British propaganda in France.

This post, combined with the strain of what was already a confirmed habit of suicidal literary industry and the pressure of theatrical commitments (Bennett became an active helper in the management of the Lyric Theatre, Hammersmith), together with attendance at dinners and parties, absorbed so much energy that a constitution never robust was seriously endangered. Sleepless nights became the rule; sleepless nights and neuralgia. In order to finish writing a play called *The Title*, 'I had to knock myself up', Bennett admitted in his *Journal*, 'and also to inform people with whom I had appointments in London that I was laid aside with a chill'.

A later entry in the *Journal* says 'Did 4 hours' hard work at the Ministry. I have now abandoned literature until I am chucked out of the job, or the job ends, or I am called to a better one. But I do journalism, and a damned nuisance it is. Two articles this week. Three next week.' And of course he had not abandoned literature. His mind was active with plays and novels then and until his final illness.

By now he had realized that it was necessary to be constantly in London; and he found it possible to retain a couple of rooms high up in the Thames Yacht Club, which he furnished in accordance with his own taste. Comfortable armchairs upholstered in an almost royal blue, a working desk of mahogany, a small table for intimate dinners, and a sense of remoteness from the traffic of Piccadilly far below are the features I remember of what seemed to be a perfect bachelor's nest. I dined there several times, and recall with amusement that on one such occasion he said blandly 'I have ventured to order our usual', which meant that we were to dine off a boiled leg of mutton accompanied by a half-bottle of champagne. I drank most of the champagne. One glass, in fact, was Bennett's allowance. If he said 'I drank too much champagne last night' he was really only saying that he had had an extra half-glass and thereby upset his digestion.

But, as will be realized, his absence from Comarques during the whole of every week did not escape Marguerite's notice. She was very lonely, having lost, it may be, even the company of 'de offissaire'. An experiment in War Work, with long hours of standing, without rest or refreshment, in some sort of kitchen, had proved too tiring, and was abandoned. Other occupations bored her. She made up her mind to investigate Arnold's situation.

A gift to the hall porter, accompanied by the mention of her name, led to discovery of the bachelor's nest. Although it was clearly not used for any improper purpose, the apartment's comfort caused her justifiable rage. While she was bored in the country, Arnold was happily occupied in London. It was intolerable. She determined that she, too, would have a *pied à terre* to which she could invite friends, and from which she could visit theatres and go to wartime parties.

Her flat was over a bank at the corner of New Oxford Street and Rathbone Place; and I was frequently invited to lunch there. I do not remember anything about its furnishing; but Bennett himself must have been a guest at her dinner parties, and only his immersion in the Great World continued to keep them apart. This work grew ever more onerous; and even at weekends, when he was occupied in writing, she saw little of him.

The fact preyed upon her mind, as I discovered one day when she was lunching with me at a restaurant. In all innocence, I asked 'How's Arnold?' To my astonishment she launched into a tirade, in French, which convulsed the other lunchers. They all, assuming that it was a violent quarrel between husband and wife, left off eating and strained their ears to attend. It was a truly embarrassing five minutes. I do not know how I managed to calm her; but the outburst died down at last, and I learned what her trouble was. It was loneliness. Hatred of his absorption in work had reached a climax.

In the end I took her back to the flat. She then insisted upon walking with me to St Martin's Lane, where I was employed; and I took her back to the flat a second time. During these walks I offered advice. It was that she should write one of her letters to Bennett, not upbraiding him, but in simple terms which would appeal to his natural reasonableness; and that she should say he was putting her in a false position, as people were beginning to assume that they had parted and were leading separate lives. In fact, that their marriage was in ruins.

We parted in good humour. Subsequently I had a note saying that she had done as I suggested, with complete success. He was to give up his cosy bachelor quarters; and they were to occupy a large flat together. This was the flat in George Street, Hanover Square which became familiar to all friends thenceforward.

Bennett never referred to this matter; and I doubt if he ever knew of my interference in his matrimonial affairs. He and I continued to meet at our Club; I frequently went to George Street; my relations with him and with Marguerite were unchanged. Only one cloud seemed to threaten complete sweetness between them; and at first I knew nothing of it.

The War had ended. The job at the Ministry of Information ceased, although it was to provide material for *Lord Raingo*. Bennett resumed to the full that concern with literature which he thought he had abandoned. But he had always, from the early days of *Polite Farces*, been full of theatrical ambition; and the success of *Milestones*, in which he had collaborated with Edward Knoblock, increased his theatrical commitments. In particular, he had become involved in the affairs of the Lyric Theatre, Hammersmith, where John Drinkwater's play about Abraham Lincoln had been a success and a new production of Gay's *The Beggar's Opera*, under Nigel Playfair's direction, drew the town.

Through this association he made another close personal friend, in Alistair ('Duff') Tayler, who was at first joined with me as Executor of his Will and later became, for a reason which I shall mention, sole Executor. Tayler was a short, agreeable Scotsman of means, who was likewise devoted to the theatre, who needed Bennett's support in what I thought, perhaps wrongly, a perpetual battle with Playfair's arbitrary courses. With these courses I had nothing to do: I judge solely by Tayler's disrespectful references.

The resumption of Bennett's domestic life with Marguerite had settled down. They were now together all the time. Unfortunately Marguerite's personality was a cause of friction which, in conjunction with the terrible habit of industry contracted in early manhood, was undermining his health. He was a sick man. I do not think she saw this; or, if she did so, she could not associate it with her own behaviour.

She had none of the vivacity which English people always expect of Frenchwomen. She did not understand, and did not like, the members of the Great World or the theatrical world whom Bennett thought it necessary to meet; and she could not adapt herself to their political sophistication or self-centred personalities. She was at ease with myself and with such other intimates as Pauline Smith and a very tall, charming young War widow named Olive Valentine, whom she envisaged as a second wife for Bennett in the event of her own death; and to us she could talk quite naturally. In other company, however, including Mrs H. G. Wells, described in front of her by Bennett as 'a great woman', she was often *distraite.* I have seen her brooding throughout a meal, resenting either the implication that Jane Wells had qualities she did not possess or the fact that all eyes turned towards Bennett, and not towards herself. Indeed, I think she suffered considerably from the neglect, sometimes the evident boredom, of those who were too much concerned with the Great World or their own profession to treat her with the considerateness they should have shown. They were not deliberately rude to her; they simply preferred Arnold. It was to see him that they came. Therefore she remained as lonely as before.

Bennett, preoccupied with his work, was patiently kind. He did his best to encourage her not very impressive gift for writing, and was delighted when she read or recited in public the poetry of Baudelaire and Albert Samain (nevertheless when at one of her public recitals she went on and on, he whispered to me, sitting beside him, and not understanding a word of the poems, 'If that damned woman doesn't hurry up we shall be late for dinner!'); and I never heard him suggest any impatience with her lugubrious tones. But he had not the time to take her to the sort of entertainment she enjoyed—highly emotional plays, for instance. I did on several occasions take her to such plays, one of them being a terrible affair called *The Prude's Fall*, by H. V. Esmond; and I had been told by E. V. Lucas that when the hero of another drama bit the heroine Marguerite exclaimed aloud 'Ah! *What* a lover!'; but I had my own girlfriends, and in the immediately post-War period there were few able-bodied young Englishmen ready to act as escorts to a middle-aged lady. It was not that she was an exacting or capricious companion; it was that she was rather heavy in hand. In my own case she seemed always to want to do the paying, an impulse, to use a phrase beloved of Trade Union leaders, which was 'entirely unacceptable' to me.

She was an inveterate letter-writer to Bennett, and Winifred Nerney sent me an enormous bundle of her correspondence which had not been destroyed. Most of the letters are in French, and begin 'mon grand cheri'; almost all of them relate trivial incidents, such as times of arrival in foreign cities, superficial impressions of individuals, the weather, her health, Arnold's health, and so on, and as a rule are free from complaints; but two, in Marguerite's English, and dated September, 1919, are rather significant. They relate to Bennett's nephew, Richard, who apparently had been staying at Comarques while his uncle was away.

'I am afraid,' she says 'you have not yet realized that Richard has not only merely been rude to me, but he has plainly made clear that he does not like me. I cannot and I *will not* look after him knowing that he distrusts me and almost hates me at times. All his behaviours since last Sunday are a proof of it. He has a strong personality—so have I—I can't begin to have serieux chills—He must be a comfort to me—or nothing else. I think he has never behave with me as he ought to since I am ill. Never he inquired about my health—does nothing for me—he has proved selfish, self-centred, is very sure that he is all right. These are things I could [not] put up with when I know he does not like me. . . . His impertinence and his attitude in his letters to me leaves no hope of him ever loving me—and I want to be loved by him like a son would. He never will.'

There is much more. I quote only one further sentence, which I think explains Marguerite's real craving, from Arnold as well as from Richard. 'My complain is such that I also need to be made fuss of, and I need affection and love.'

Naturally Arnold's friends were Arnold's friends. He was much loved. Men as different as Maugham and Max Beerbohm always referred to him as 'dear Arnold', and were greatly concerned for his health and his happiness. This was a general attachment, not accorded to Marguerite. In a letter which I have not quoted she says, referring again to the trouble with Richard, that he has said definitely that when his uncle was away he was unhappy to be with Marguerite alone. It was Bennett's pervading good humour that made the atmosphere of their home agreeable.

Marguerite refers to her illness. This illness was genuine. Apparently she had some chest trouble in 1918 and 1919 that alarmed her and even led to a short period in a nursing home. But Arnold's friends knew nothing of her anxiety. I do not remember hearing about it myself, although I may have done so. What I remember is that there was much concern among men who saw him from time to time over the evident deterioration in his vitality; and on one occasion when Edward Knoblock and I had been lunching with both Bennetts we walked away in a state of depression. Knoblock suddenly exclaimed 'Arnold's very ill. She gives him no peace. If you don't get him away from her for a complete rest, he'll die.' Staggered by this demand, I said 'I? I can't do anything.' Knoblock replied 'Yes, you can. You're the only person who can.'

Now I have never tried to 'win friends and influence' anybody. I was born cheerful, talkative, and independent; but I have never been in the habit, as some men are, especially if they come from Yorkshire or Lancashire, of giving unasked advice. But when one's duty is pointed out, even if it is unpleasant, some disturbance arises in the mind, or the moral sense. It was clear that Knoblock had no use for Marguerite (I was told he was not interested in women at all); but it had also been clear during luncheon that Bennett was completely exhausted. His movements and responses were slow. He kept looking round him as if in silent despair. And Marguerite had been truculent, a fact which had produced a further weary silence.

Work, work, work, involvement in the affairs of others (C. F. G. Masterman, for instance, said to Mrs Masterman, 'if you're in serious trouble, go to Arnold Bennett. He's the one') and all sorts of business complications, coupled with a lack of tranquillity at home, had beaten him at last. He was at the end of his strength.

Feeling this, and being called on by Knoblock to take some step, I felt compelled to overcome natural congenital dislike of meddling. Taking the opportunity, therefore, of sitting beside him while we were lunching with other men at the Reform Club, I made the venture. I said 'You really ought to get away for a complete change.' He nodded gloomily. 'I know. But it's no fun going alone.' Having an extremely indulgent boss in Percy Spalding, senior partner in the firm of Chatto & Windus, whose affection for me had been shown in many ways, I took his consent to my absence for granted, and said 'I'll go with you.' Bennett jumped. 'Will you? Would you go to Portugal? Oh, but that's splendid!'

Rising instantly, he went down the dining-room to another table, at which the head of the Booth Line, whom I did not know, was sitting. Within minutes he was back again, having arranged for our passage to Lisbon on a Booth liner. He was jubilant. I have never seen, in anybody, so rapid a change of mood.

There was a curious sequel to this transaction. While I still rejoiced at the simplicity and promise of the arrangement I was confronted by Marguerite in a state of furious anger, and severely rated for malign interference in her affairs. 'I 'ave been telling Arnole for months that he need a 'oliday. He take no notice. No notice whatever. But when *you* say it he agree at once. He *always* do what you wish!'

This was absurd, of course; an outburst of sudden jealousy. But it put me in a dilemma. I could not reveal the fact that what his friends thought necessary was escape from herself. Nor could I abandon the agreement he and I had reached about a holiday in Portugal. At this distance of time, nearly sixty years later, I do not remember what I said in self-defence. Probably I expressed strong sympathy with herself, which I felt; but I expect I offered a guarantee to bring him back restored to complete health. Whatever I said must have been convincing; for in spite of her previous sense of outrage she grew calm; and we parted on good terms once more.

6

Bennett and I sailed from Liverpool aboard R.M.S. *Hildebrand* on January 30th, 1920. She was a good ship, with a bearded Irish captain at whose table we sat for the voyage. We heard many interesting observations from him about the world in general, together with a rather drastic proposal for the solution of Irish affairs. This was that the island should be scuttled in mid-Atlantic.

Once on board ship Bennett, with the sniff of salt water in his nostrils, became a different man. We walked together along the ample decks in a state of enthusiasm; and as night fell we enjoyed a fascinating experience—the dropping of our pilot. This, for Bennett, ravished by such phenomena, was pure magic. First we saw below us a movement in the ship's side from which a great beam of light suddenly shone. The beam soon revealed a tiny boat in the darkness below. A figure went down backwards from the ship by rope ladder. We were breathless as he dropped safely into the boat; but we laughed also, because in the midst of the dramatic scene, with black sea all around the single beam of light, we could perceive that the pilot wore a bowler hat. A shout or two; the boat pulled away; the beam was extinguished. Bennett's satisfaction was immense. Our journey could not have had a better beginning.

The *Hildebrand* rounded the Cornish coast and passed up the Channel to le Havre, where we went ashore and walked about the streets and quays. Here again Bennett was happy, as he always was when at sea or at a port. He loved to watch ships coming and going, as he loved precise punctuality. I remember that once, when H. W. Massingham, editor of *The Nation*, and I were on his second, much grander, yacht, the *Marie Marguerite*, Massingham and I went for a walk in Dover on the Sunday morning, and saw what we thought to be a succession of remarkable things, from Swedish sailors unloading timber to a Dance Hall with the notice 'No Dogs Admitted'. Massingham remarked 'Won't Arnold be sorry he didn't come with us!' I said 'No. We shall tell him what we've seen, and he'll say "That . . . is nothing at all. *I* have seen the Calais boat come in".' My prophecy came true to the very words, with the addition 'exactly to time'.

Massingham, the only man I have known of whom it could truthfully be said, 'doubled up with laughter'. He had not realized, as I did, Bennett's pride in British seamanship and pleasure in the beautiful sight of a cross-Channel boat tossing aside the spray as it entered harbour.

We were in the bow of the *Hildebrand* when she left le Havre, and we were able to be on deck, where there was dancing at night, during the passage across an equable Bay of Biscay. The weather was uniformly fine throughout our voyage. I recall watching the coastline, and arrival in the palm-studded port of Leixoes (pronounced Lishoens), and as at that time I had never been farther from England than Paris and Brussels I was enchanted. Even Bennett, with much greater experience, gave the scene an approving nod.

We went by hired car for a day in Oporto, spending lavishly on an exchange rate then ridiculously in favour of the British pound; and left in the evening for our final destination, Lisbon. The sight of that city from the Tagus is breathtaking—or was so to a novice—with pastel-coloured buildings rising from the water's edge and the brilliant sunshine giving the reality the glory of a travel agent's brochure. I see it now as I saw it nearly sixty years ago, and realize that while the object of the journey was a restoration of Bennett's health a less important detail was my own sensational enrichment.

We went directly from Lisbon to Mont Estoril, on the Portuguese Riviera, where we met a Mr Radcliffe, owner of a Liverpool newspaper, and his daughter, together with members of the map-making firm of Bartholomew. These were our companions in the evenings, where I remember that a primitive kind of roulette was sometimes played—always, in spite of an indulgent croupier, to our loss. During the day we took long walks, or drives in a horse-drawn fly. The driver of this fly must have been one of the oldest men in Portugal, with whom Bennett had fluent conversations in an unknown lingo. I marvelled at their loquacity, and asked Bennett what the magic was that enabled such a relationship to occur. He answered blandly, 'a mixture of French and Latin'. The mixture was evidently quite intelligible, for the old man never made a mistake, and took us wherever we wanted to go.

On the very first morning after our arrival, Bennett came down to breakfast with a familiar announcement. 'I have . . . written six hundred words this morning.' I cried 'Oh! Oh! Oh! What about your promise to do no work?' His guilty 'I know. I *had* to' was a sign that the leopard cannot change its spots.

He had to write. If he was not starting or finishing a novel or a play, he was writing articles or short stories or entries in his copious *Journal*, or letters of immense length. It was a disease. All the same, for the rest of our stay in Portugal I heard no more boasts; and I gathered when I read the printed *Journal* many years later that after this first lapse he kept his word. The entry for March 9th, 1920 is 'I went with Swinnerton on a month's holiday to Portugal on Jan 29, and returned last Wednesday, March 3rd.'

When we had been at Mont Estoril for a few days, an imposing lady, said to be a connection of Arthur Pinero, the dramatist, came to our table and asked Bennett to support some *fête* or entertainment which she was organizing. He had to sign a form; and the lady demanded 'Are you *the* Arnold Bennett?' He said, with fortitude, 'I . . . believe so', and she went away. Later I was told that she made merry (I suspect because she would have liked to boast of acquaintance with him) over our solemn, speechless promenades together; but she was quite wrong about the solemnity. We may have appeared speechless to a jaundiced eye. In fact we had a good deal of conversation.

It was not philosophic. When I mentioned that I had read Evelyn Underhill's book on mysticism, he said 'There's nothing in mysticism'. Nor was it heart-to-heart, neither of us being given to self-examination. On the contrary, it was objective. We both knew a number of the same people, from Wells to Hugh Walpole, and we were published in the United States by a superb 'character', George Doran, an Irish Canadian, who believed himself to be one of Bennett's most intimate friends. There were several of such men, including Newman Flower, who edited three volumes of the *Journal.* I made no similar claim. I always take what the Gods send, in friendship as in life.

This was one of our bonds. We could discuss other men with affectionate detachment. Hugh Walpole, for instance, whom Bennett called 'Hughie' and Ellen Glasgow, 'apple-cheeked Hugh'. We were fond of Walpole, as I think were most of those who knew him; but we found some of his manifestations a matter for non-malicious laughter.

Walpole's personality was a curious mixture. It united a capacity for ardent affection with unsleeping distrust and a treachery usually associated with cats. Knowing my propensity for disrespectful anecdote, he said he did not mind what I said about him, as long as I made it clear that he was my friend. Whether he made the same compact with Bennett, I do not know; but there was a dark side to his sunny temperament, and we were both accused of faults in his private papers, as is revealed in Hart-Davis's biography. There Bennett was charged with egotism, and I with 'untrustworthiness'. It did not matter. We were sportive about him, as about Doran and others.

From time to time Bennett communicated various examples of his dogmatic *obiter dicta,* of which I never discovered the sources. Some, I thought, might have been drawn from Tupper's *Proverbial Philosophy,* others from Staffordshire local-lore, others again from his own essentially comic vision. I remember 'Nine out of ten people improve on acquaintance', 'Only a small man needs to stand on his dignity', and 'A dirty mind is a continual feast'; but there were many more, as to which we never argued.

In those days I was said to be a good mimic; and I made Bennett smile by my impersonations of present and former bosses, Percy Spalding and J. M. Dent, both publishers. The one a darling, who, when we both retired from the firm, signed his letters 'Yours everly, Per', the other an irritable and occasionally noisy tyrant who told me I must 'devolve' my work, spoke of things being 'insiduous' or 'insinuous', and once sent an instruction to his senior traveller 'do not let the ground grow under your feet'. Furthermore, we often exchanged quite silly little jokes, one of which occurs to me as I write. It arose when our antique coachman took us to Cintra.

We were driving into the celebrated Garden when I saw an unexpectedly familiar sight. I exclaimed 'Good heavens! I've seen a picture of this vista painted by the worst artist in the world!' Bennett asked 'And who is the worst artist in the world?' I told him, 'Stanley Inchbold', and he said 'Oh, no, he's not the worst artist in the world. The worst artist in the world is my old friend Frederick Marriott'. (It was to this friend that he dedicated *A Great Man*, with 'the imperishable memory of old times'). I digested the information. Then, remembering the dreadful individual performance of a man at Bennett's Lyric Theatre who based his diction on that of Henry Irving, and made every 'd' a 't', I said 'I'd tell you who is the worst *actor* in the world, only you'd contradict me'. 'And who is the worst actor in the world?' I told him. 'Well,' responded Bennett; 'he *is*.'

It was this sportiveness that characterized our talk. He was, in the modern phrase, 'completely relaxed', with no exhausting parties to attend, no books or plays to plan and write, no deadlines to keep, no complaints to endure, and no family or other responsibilities to shoulder. The holiday gave him exercise and refreshed his mind. Marguerite, handsomely admitting this, told me that when they had dropped me outside my Bloomsbury flat Bennett said 'Do you know, that chap hasn't worried me once all the time we've been away'.

This reported compliment may have been true; but the holiday had been merely a lighthearted 'frolic', as he would once have called it. To my mind the remark was a saddening admission that his once-resolute Stoicism was failing. At fifty-three he had been thankful to find understanding companionship in a man seventeen years his junior, whose sole positive assets were humour and loquacity. I believe he had ceased, and knew himself to have ceased, to be the self-assured Enoch Arnold who had viewed Time as his inspiration. *The Old Wives' Tale* and *Clayhanger* lay behind. They were never to be equalled as great adventures. Of serious novels only *Riceyman Steps*, derived from a little work about misers picked up in a Southampton bookshop, and *Lord Raingo*, drawn from his experience at the Ministry of Information, lay ahead. He still had wonderful resources of insight and talent; but the last ten years of his life were to be years of increasing trial.

7

I do not now remember when the young Frenchman, René le Gros, entered the Bennett circle. My impression is that he may have been a relative of Marguerite's; but this is only an impression. He was said to be a teacher of French at an English college for women; was a small man without marked personality; and always, most respectfully, addressed his host and hostess as 'Monsieur' and 'Madame'. I met him only two or three times, and as far as I recollect had no personal conversation with him.

At the time, I was considerably preoccupied with my own affairs. My mother, dependent on me, had become an invalid, and was in successive nursing-homes, which I had constantly to visit; an aunt, her sister, partly dependent, was being extremely difficult; and I was in love. Bennett and I, for the most part, met at luncheon at our Club, where the company—of journalists, magistrates, economists, and Members of Parliament—indulged in the best talk I have ever heard and we were both treated with warm cordiality by all—including the waiters. Marguerite and I sometimes lunched together, at restaurants when I was host, at her Club, where Bennett pretended that the women members all drank liqueurs before lunch, when she could satisfy her wish to pay the bill.

I mention the payment of the bill for a reason which will be clear in a moment and which will link up with the opening words of the chapter. But I must make it clear that I still occasionally dined in the Bennetts' big flat in George Street, Hanover Square, where they continued to entertain all sorts of men and women, and where I met Monsieur le Gros. Their lives appeared to be normal.

And then, one day, Bennett telephoned, asking if he could come along to my flat in Bloomsbury. This was an entirely unprecedented visit, and the only explanation he gave on the telephone was that he wanted to see me on a matter of importance. He came, looking very serious, refused any refreshment, and sat down in an armchair. I ought perhaps to mention that I rented this handsomely furnished but rather dusty flat from Bertrand Russell, and that when I first met Lady Ottoline Morrell she greeted me by saying 'Oh, you live in Bertie's flat, don't you? Has it still got the furniture I bought for him?' Bennett ignored the furnishing: he was concerned with something so grave that I doubt if he noticed it. All he said about the place was 'You ought to have some flowers here'.

The object of his visit was to tell me that Marguerite had announced her intention of leaving him. He said she had threatened to go several times before; but had withdrawn the threat. This time, under provocation, he had advised her to see a solicitor who would arrange a legal separation. He was very much disturbed, saying more than once 'I married her for life'. The name of René le Gros was mentioned; and I said I did not believe the association to be an amorous one. I asked Bennett if he agreed; and he answered that he did. Nevertheless I am in possession of a typed letter from le Gros, dated in June 1921, answering one from Bennett, protesting in terms of injured innocence that both he and Marguerite had behaved throughout with complete propriety and great circumspectness.

My view was, and is, that Marguerite, needing companionship and, as she put it in the letter about Richard, 'a fuss' made of her, had welcomed the coming of le Gros, who had the same need. This must have been the truth. He, after all, was a stranger in London, and the Bennett home was a haven for him. I think Marguerite, who had wanted Richard to be like a son to her, saw in le Gros the equivalent of her desired son. It has been stated that Bennett denied her children because of some insanity in her family. It has also been stated, in a Press interview, by his sister, Mrs Beardmore, that he refused to have children because they would interfere with his work. Neither explanation was ever given to myself. All I know is that Marguerite installed le Gros in the flat she vacated when she and Bennett went together to George Street, took him to Bennett's expensive tailors, paid his bills, and at last found the dress allowance she received from Bennett insufficient to meet all her new expenses.

She therefore said 'Now, Arnole, you 'ave been giving me seven 'undred pounds a year. In future it must be fifteen 'undred'. According to Bennett, his reply was 'If I am to give you fifteen hundred, I must sell either Comarques or the yacht'. Marguerite's angry answer to what sounded like a characteristically moderate Arnoldian response to her demand was 'I shall leave you'. 'Then,' said Bennett, 'you should see a solicitor'.

It was the first time he had ever said such a thing to her.

I was naturally much distressed by what I heard, and gave all the understanding and sympathy I could to a friend who was incapable of emotional display. I felt he was deeply unhappy not only at the quarrel, but at having to confess inability to deal with a domestic situation. His need to confide in somebody whom he thought trustworthy proved indeed that, as I suggested earlier, his self-assurance was failing.

What followed put me once again in a dilemma; for within a few days Marguerite supplied her version of what had happened. She asked me urgently to lunch at her Club, and poured out a vehement tale of wrongs and long-suffering. According to her, she had asked reasonably for an increase in her allowance; and Arnold had refused point blank. At this, greatly offended, she had retorted 'You are a rackscal!' (but Bennett later contradicted this, saying 'She called me the worst there is in French. She called me a dirty dog!') Marguerite added, to me, 'For fourteen years it has been "Arnole! Arnole! Arnole!" ' Now, she said, she was finished with him.

No reference was made in her story to le Gros. Her agitation was concerned only with Bennett's parsimony, and the fact that her life with him had been one of constant self-sacrifice. 'Fourteen years! Fourteen years!' Naturally, I could not mention the different account I had heard from Bennett; and I professed all the sympathy I felt with a distraught woman. I assumed that this trouble would pass, as previous threats of separation had done. But Bennett's 'you should see a solicitor' had been fatal. She had seen a solicitor.

I learned later that two separate English solicitors had told her to accept proposals made on Bennett's behalf for her future maintenance. Always interested in money, she rejected these proposals as inadequate, and demanded larger and larger sums. It was not until she went to a French solicitor that she was given backing for her claim; and in the end she accepted two thousand pounds a year, without tax deduction, provided that Bennett's income did not fall below a certain amount. If it did so, the allowance was to be adjusted proportionately. She was warned that her protracted haggling, by making Bennett ill and incapable of work, was already lessening this amount (and therefore her own contingent and proportionate expectation) by a thousand pounds a month. She settled.

Marguerite was still at the George Street flat when I dined there alone with Bennett; but she did not appear. Instead, she remained in her room. It was then that I heard the only harsh words Bennett ever spoke of her. He was silent for a long time during the meal; but after this silence he suddenly exclaimed 'To think of that poor middle-aged fool, sitting there, thinking . . . all sorts of things!' That was all; and he never again referred to her.

I have thought of the matter a great deal in the intervening years; and if I now write dispassionately (I am quite sure of the words spoken on both sides, because I can still hear them in memory) it is because I am a very old man, happily married for more than half a century to a dear and ever-considerate wife. Bennett liked and respected my wife very much, and did so from their first meeting. If Marguerite had been such a wife no parting would have taken place. She had no rival. 'I married her for life,' said Bennett. At heart he was a Puritan, as well as a Stoic; and his integrity was instinctive.

This is not to say that Puritans and Stoics make ideal husbands for those who 'need to have a fuss' made of them; and my wife insists that Bennett was not, and never had been, in love with Marguerite. On the other hand I am convinced that Marguerite had no real intention of leaving him. I think she was carried by excitement into excessive vehemence, and that his dogged refusal to answer in similar terms made it impossible for her to withdraw the threat. It must be remembered that if he had been living under great strain she had been doing the same in a different way, especially during the War and in what was in many ways an alien atmosphere. The humble and admiring le Gros recalled France, aroused her maternal longings for a son's love, and produced a belief that she had suffered lifelong frustration. No wonder she was thinking 'all sorts of things!'

There was something else, too. Richard had confessed that he did not like her. It was a great shock. What if others felt as Richard did? In this mood of angry wretchedness she concluded that Bennett's English friends also found her a tiresome and moody creature with nothing to offer of amusement or stimulation. The 'great' ones were full of their own worldly affairs; the smaller fry too obviously gave adulation to her husband. Nobody confided in her or flattered her; nobody made a 'fuss' of her. They took her for granted. These were very bitter thoughts indeed.

From the moment she left Bennett, Marguerite was dropped by those who, by their kindness, might have sustained her. They did not quarrel. They simply, with one or two exceptions, who included his sister Tertia, possibly Mrs Belloc Lowndes, and I hope myself, discontinued contact with her. After a short time she returned to France, where she took pride in the fact that she was referred to as 'Madame l'Anglaise', made a few visits to England, staying with Tertia; but for the most part remained at home. And from that time onward she signed her letters, even to me, 'Marguerite Arnold Bennett'. I have no doubt at all—in fact she admits this in her poor little book *My Arnold Bennett*—that until his death she hoped for a reconciliation.

8

With Marguerite's departure, Bennett resumed a bachelor life. He gave up the flat in George Street, taking a house in Cadogan Square, Chelsea, and interesting himself in the ordering of his establishment.

He furnished his drawing-room completely in Victorian style, even, I believe, to a table centrepiece of wax flowers under a bulbous glass case, and causing purists to exclaim at, and ridicule his taste. But he entertained on a great scale, having guests as unlike each other as Beaverbrook, George Doran, Maurice Baring, Lytton Strachey, and Margaret Kennedy to dinner, and constituting himself a sort of literary uncle to Siegfied Sassoon, Aldous Huxley, Middleton Murry, W. J. Turner, and the Sitwells. I attended a few of these parties, and did not scorn the Victorian furniture, because I thought it suited Bennett much better than his old Empire suites and the mirror-panelled doors, not of his own installation, of his new home.

Harriet Cohen and other musicians came to play and sing; and Harriet Cohen enabled him to indulge his love of playing pianoforte duets. He bought a wonderful gramophone, which he proudly played when Mrs H. G. Wells and I were his sole guests. Mrs Wells and I were tremendously impressed, and as the recital ended she said politely 'I suppose that's one of the best there is.' Bennett replied 'It *is* the best'.

This reminds me that I have heard him say, with humour, 'The best is good enough for me'. The remark was repeated as '*Only* the best is good enough for me'—a piece of snobbery impossible to one who was never guilty of the vice. It associated him, quite wrongly, with those who were accustomed to say that they cared only for 'the first class'. Aldous Huxley ridiculed the pretentiousness in *Crome Yellow*, when Mary finds

Anne reading in bed, looks at the book, and comments 'Rather second-rate, isn't it?' Huxley's supplementary remark is 'The tone in which Mary pronounced the word "second-rate" implied an almost infinite denigration. She was accustomed to associate only with first-rate people who liked first-rate things, and she knew that there were very, very few first-rate things in the world, and that what there were were mostly French'.

It is not surprising that Huxley was condemned as an ephemeral writer by those who cared only for the first-class. Curiously enough, I never heard Bennett use the term 'second-rate'. His standards were high; but his taste was catholic. Of scamped or pretentious work his description was less snobbish. He said, tersely 'No good'.

At this time he began to put on weight, a fact which David Low seized upon in an amusing but very malicious and damaging caricature. The caricature showed him as a pot-bellied and exceedingly prosperous man from the North; and it enabled those who wished to offer themselves as the apostles of fine taste to accuse him of being a vulgarian who 'simply stank of brass'. It was an injustice; but it impressed the immediately post-War generation.

I do not wish to involve myself in literary polemics; and I shall not pursue this matter further. I merely remark that the injustice followed previous lines—the gaping provincial, the man who planned to write pot-boilers to the age of forty and then marry a French wife and write a masterpiece, and, with boasts of his earnings, 'took the cash and let the credit go'. During the War he had written much journalism, and his name had been displayed in posters on the front of omnibuses. Beaverbrook, whose belief in publicity was measureless, had made him 'news'. His very occasional presence at theatrical first nights, and his air of always wearing his 'Sunday best', led to the report that besides wearing a frilled dress shirt (which I think was true) he had actually been seen in one of a bright pink. He figured in a *revue*, saying 'Well, I must have a sleep.' And literary dandies discovered that his deliberately plain manner of writing was a sign of mediocrity.

Those who knew him well loved and were amused by Bennett. Those who did not know him were offended by his oracular statements. They did not dream that, as I suspect, the oracular statements arose from his stammer, which made him jerk out a few words and return to silence.

On the subject of this silence, I venture to record a personal anecdote which may be misrepresented. Our literary agent at this time, Eric Pinker, once asked me to dinner, saying that he had a number of bores coming and would like me to join them. I reported the invitation to Bennett with laughing indignation; and he said 'That reminds me, can you come to dinner on Friday?' I protested, still laughing; whereupon Bennett replied, seriously, and very confidentially, 'When I have anybody coming that I'm . . . not sure of, I like to have *you* there.'

I do not remember how many people he was 'not sure of'; but I suppose them to have been those who for one reason or another would cause his stammer to be uncontrollable. As I have said before, I do not stammer, and he had great trust in me as one who understood him and could not be intimidated by rudeness or conversational fireworks. Two possible names occur to me at this moment, those of James Agate, who could be noisy and aggressive, and Osbert Sitwell, whose sister, Dame Edith, told Bennett that he was always playing practical jokes, and who certainly would not be easy for a stammerer to deal with as a solitary guest. I say this because I was at a lunch given by Bennett, when Osbert made merciless attacks on Siegfried Sassoon, who admitted to being 'er, quite an ordinary chap' and, although capable of satire in verse, had no power of repartee. It was a disagreeable lunch, which might have ended in a quarrel if Bennett, perhaps fortified by my presence, had not intervened and made them part friends.

The increase in weight clearly troubled him; and he sought the advice of his friend Dr Shufflebotham. 'Shuf' suggested that he should take up dancing. Having no lightness of foot, he could not be a good dancer, and at least one of his partners, Mrs St John Ervine, told me that when they began she felt her heart sink. However, his love of precision came to the rescue, and he hummed all the tunes, so that the evening passed without too great discomfort. He danced whenever possible, in London, on the Riviera, and elsewhere; but whether this had any real effect upon his weight I cannot say. The weight was reduced; he became much slimmer; and in his later years, still walking with stiff shoulders, he was back to a normal size. One result of this was his play, *The Return Journey*, which was a version of the Faust legend.

Association with the Lyric Theatre, Hammersmith, led to Bennett's ever deeper absorption in his old craft of play-writing. He had had a great success with *Milestones*, invented by Edward Knoblock but entirely written, he told me, by himself. *The Great Adventure*, a dramatization of *Buried Alive*, was also a great success; but although three or four others, including *The Title* and *Sacred and Profane Love*, had respectable runs none of them was very good, and like other dramatists Bennett had difficulty in getting what he wrote produced. One at least, *The Bright Island*, was done at the Lyric, and another, *The Love Match*, had important consequences in his personal life. The most ambitious of all, *Dòn Juan de Marana*, was a cause of serious tribulation. Matheson Lang was willing to play in it on his own terms; but negotiations fell through. Other managers were not even interested in the script.

Towards the end of 1923 I went to the United States on a lecture tour. This was quite a usual thing to do at the time, for American readers were curious to see British authors. Hugh Walpole toured several times, and with his mixture of humour and boyish earnestness was exceedingly successful. Lord Dunsany, arrogant and peremptory, was less liked. American authors, from Joseph Hergesheimer to Sinclair Lewis, although I was told Hergesheimer was 'too ugly' and Lewis 'too rude' to please audiences were often on the platform. Doran hoped for better results from me.

I was away for more than three and a half months, leaving England on November 23rd, 1923. During the tour I travelled to New England, the Middle West, South to Georgia, West to California, from Pasadena to San Francisco, North again to Oregon and Montana, South again to Alabama, where the Montgomery newspaper, by headlining me 'just folks', brought a packed house to the local theatre, and so once more to New York. Home again by March 15th, 1924, and full of rich memories, I was married that very day, and have 'lived happy ever after'.

Before going to America, however, I had bought for £2,350 a most attractive Elizabethan cottage in the country; and Bennett paid me a visit there. He referred to this cottage in a letter to somebody else as 'Swinnerton's rural wigwam', and told friends that I had paid too much for it. This was not the case. Old Tokefield, Cranleigh, Surrey, had been ingeniously converted from three small cottages by an artist named Lawson Wood, whose hobby it was to make similar conversions, and it has proved a very happy home for over half a century.

Indeed my wife and I have experienced only one lasting sorrow during our occupation, the loss of our elder daughter through injury at birth. It has enabled us to offer hospitality to friends, is now rated at over four hundred pounds a year, and is being up-graded from a dwelling of local interest to one of national interest. Bennett was therefore wrong about it; his doubt of my wisdom was merely an expression of anxiety for a friend's wellbeing.

While inviting himself for this brief visit he mentioned that he would like to bring a young actress who had appeared in the Liverpool production of his play, *The Love Match.* He said he hoped I would find her, in Doctor Johnson's phrase, 'not unclubbable.' I had taken possession of the cottage on March 23rd, and having disliked Lawson Wood's Elizabethan 'period' forms and uncomfortable chairs, had furnished it largely from Heals with an eye to elegant ease. Bennett and his actress friend came for tea on Whit Monday, May 21st. This was the day, therefore, on which I made a first acquaintance with Dorothy Cheston, who lived with Bennett until his death eight years later.

She was a dazzling blonde, of a nature altogether different from Marguerite. She had immense energy, plenty to say for herself, and a command of long words surpassing anything I have known in man or woman. No reference was made to her relations with Bennett, no endearments passed between them, and they left in good time and good order. The only event I really remember is that in too unwarily entering the scullery, where he had no business, Bennett bumped his head against the low lintel, uttering the only reproof he ever addressed to me. This was 'You ought to have told me', a complaint which, having bumped my own head many times on his yachts, I wholly rejected.

I was told later by Alistair Tayler, who eventually became sole executor of Bennett's will (although at that time he and I were joint executors), of a strange incident relating to Dorothy.

He had accompanied Bennett on the Liverpool excursion, and they had consorted with members of the repertory company which was giving *The Love Match.* As the two men were about to return to London, Bennett said urgently 'Duff, you must stick closely to me. *She* is coming to see us off.'

You remember that he had said 'When I have somebody coming that I'm not . . . sure of, I like to have you there'. I was not available. Tayler, a very amiable man, who had none of my protective coolness, was the only alternative available. The reference to Miss Cheston as 'she' was no more than a characteristic preference for a pronoun. In the light of what happened afterwards it assumed a meaning which I am sure Bennett did not intend.

9

The first of the two World Wars had brought great changes to the literary scene. Thomas Hardy's reputation as a novelist gave place to a new reputation, not sustained, as a poet. George Moore ceased to be the realist of *Esther Waters* (which some thought an imitation of Hardy's *Tess*) and *A Mummer's Wife*, and converted himself into a re-teller of religious or classical histories. Wells, Galsworthy, and Bennett were assuming the aspect of past masters. The novelists who had just arrived before the War, Compton Mackenzie, Hugh Walpole, Gilbert Cannan, J. D. Beresford, Rose Macaulay, E. M. Forster, Oliver Onions, and Sheila Kaye-Smith, who followed earlier examples were expected to go on as before, adjusting themselves to a re-settled world.

They could not do this. It is now said that they had not assimilated the teachings of Marx and Freud, of whom the first taught that individuals were small items in a human mass, and the latter small collections of motives and desires. This failure to notice the scientific trend explains a certain eclipse in reputation, which for most of them continues until today. Curiously enough, Somerset Maugham, denounced in those days as 'a mere storyteller', crept into fame and fortune, and began to be found rather better than before.

On the outbreak of War, critical writers such as E. B. Osborn, who had always disliked realism, and felt that R. L. Stevenson and his fellow-exponents of swordsmanship and the picturesque represented an ideal, announced that blood and glory would produce a new heroic literature. It was assumed that the War would be short, full of cavalry charges and opposed chivalries, with victory falling to the indomitable British; and when ardent young poets, Julian Grenfell, Rupert Brooke, Siegfried Sassoon, Robert Graves, and Robert Nichols, with Gilbert Frankau as Kiplingesque drum-beater, went into the Army they seemed to bring the prospect of new life to a craft which, dominated by Robert Bridges, had come to be, however noble in spirit and rhythms, at heart unsustained by ecstasy.

The poets were not the only British writers to go to the War. They were joined by novelists like Compton Mackenzie, who preferred to express his reaction to it in volumes of reminiscence, A. P. Herbert, who wrote of it poignantly in *The Secret Battle*, Richard Aldington, and R. H. Mottram, and by journalists like C. E. Montague, H. W. Nevinson, H. M. Tomlinson, and Philip Gibbs, all of whom in the end had grimmer stories to tell than the optimistic prophets had imagined. The effect was to introduce a new pessimism into modern literature. Montague called his account of the fighting *Disenchantment*, while Tomlinson's inevitable war-novel was *All Our Yesterdays*.

Some of the poets, while still singing, lost their lives. Others lived to write bitterly of the incompetence of commanders and the foulness of War. Older men—Wells and Bennett among them—visited the Western Front without experience of the fighting. What they wrote had, therefore, only ephemeral interest. Wells's verbal account of being raced across open ground between the trenches by his escort, C. E. Montague, with the remark that 'the other lot will all have their heads down', held all his mischievous fun; Bennett's *Over There* was no more than reprinted journalism in which he recorded the sights, sounds, and contacts of a hasty tour. The real thing was very different.

My closest friend, P. P. Howe, the editor and biographer of Hazlitt, who went all through the War, referred to it as unending nightmare, and would never speak of his experiences at all. The others, Mottram, Aldington, Tomlinson, Montague, and Philip Gibbs, and the poets Sassoon, Robert Graves, Wilfred Owen, wrote and spoke more freely; but for the most part only after the War was over, and there were other men who for one reason or another did not take part in the fighting and did not see—until long afterwards—the varying scenes in which it took place. I was one of these men.

As I have mentioned earlier, I was seriously ill in the early months of the War, and even when compulsory military service was introduced with the object of replacing immense casualties on the Somme and elsewhere (two of P. P. Howe's brothers, both highly talented boys, typical of their idealistic generation, were killed on the Somme) I was not called up. I was summoned for a medical examination, found unfit, and dismissed, a fact which now that I am in my 94th year seems unbelievable. Others, long dead from natural causes, were absorbed by the Army. My brother, non-combative by nature, served in three different regiments, two of them kilted, but always in England.

The Act imposing compulsory service contained a stipulation that those who had conscientious scruples about taking life could be excused. Many were given what was called 'alternative service', but all had to appear before small tribunals composed of older men. If they were not exempted they had a right of appeal to a higher body. I was asked by a friend to testify to his genuineness as an 'objector', and I therefore attended one of the Appeals Tribunals on his behalf. This friend was an ascetic scholar named Clement Miles, who had written a learned but to me unreadable book on the celebration of Christmas in all ages and countries. Knowledge that he could no more handle a rifle than a child of four, I agreed to give my testimony.

I therefore sat through one of the most painful days I have ever experienced. My friend's case was not reached that day, and before it could come on again he had died of anaemia; but I heard a number of youngsters being questioned, and was sickened by a great deal of the evidence. Much of it was given by agitated girl friends who swore that the applicants had always expressed horror at the thought of killing; and the Chairman of the Tribunal, a barrister and Liberal M.P. showed an anxious wish to be fair to all. The proceedings, however, were stammering and for the most part futile.

And then there came a sudden change. A small, heavily bearded man with the voice of a lambkin was ushered to the appointed seat. He was accompanied by two men who nodded to the Chairman with obvious familiarity and sat down with none of the fear and embarrassment shown by previous witnesses. I shall not mention the name of the small bearded man, who is dead. I shall say only that he belonged to that body of intellectuals whom Bennett always called, with irony, 'the élite'.

There was no suggestion that he was a coward. He was simply one of those young men of his generation who regarded War as uncivilized barbarism and refused to take any part in it. He was not asked about his conscientious objection; his sponsors assured the Chairman that he had always been rather eccentric in his views and conduct; and when the Chairman inquired if there was any War in which he would be willing to take part he bleated that if one arose in which black warriors strove to destroy white communities he would resist them. The Chairman had a whispered consultation with his colleagues, and reached a prompt decision. 'As the object of the Act is to enlist soldiers for *this* War,' he said, 'we grant your exemption.' Glaring on the assembled company, he added 'And if anyone questions our decision, he can take the matter to a higher Court.'

Nobody, of course, thought of doing that. The trio left the Court as they had entered it, leaving at least one of the auditors in some perturbation. When I next saw my friend Miles he was in hospital, unable to recognize me, while an ether spray eased his passage into a realm where War, I hope, is unknown.

I should not have inflicted this story upon the reader if it had not illustrated a tendency of that particular period. It was the coming into prominence of a small body of people which has been known, not always accurately, as Bloomsbury.

The High Priestess of this body was Virginia Woolf, the daughter of an influential Victorian critic named Leslie Stephen who edited *The Dictionary of National Biography* and wrote, among many other books, *A History of English Thought in the Eighteenth Century*. Having announced to the world that human nature changed round about the year 1910, Virginia Woolf contributed to T. S. Eliot's critical review, *The Criterion*, a paper on the Georgian Novelists, whom she named as James Joyce (but in a less public comment she likened *Ulysses* to 'a queasy undergraduate scratching his pimples'), E. M. Forster, Lytton Strachey, D. H. Lawrence, and T. S. Eliot. She remarked that she would not cross the street in order to meet Charles Dickens; and expressed contempt for Henry James. Wells, Galsworthy, and Bennett also met with her disapproval, and in a pamphlet entitled *Mr Bennett and Mrs Brown* she made great fun of Bennett's detailed method of introducing characters and telling a story.

This attack set the tone for much adverse comment on Bennett, superseding the earlier attacks on his provinciality and bedazzlement by splendour. He was accused of being 'commercial' and of 'selling the pass' to mediocrity. But Bennett had a dogma regarding the Novel as a species of literature. He insisted that mastery of it consisted in the ability to create living characters; and Virginia Woolf, who admitted that, being self-absorbed, she never knew what other people were thinking, did not create living characters. Her method was called 'the stream of consciousness', and it demanded a certain amount of intellectual conceit in its appreciative readers.

Fashion has changed since the nineteen-twenties. Another War has been fought; women have lost their mysteriousness for men and become much more active in public affairs; and the most popular of today's novels, apart from the theatrical biographies of 'anti-heroes', are about fornication, rape, homosexual relationships, guns and spies, or about the recognizable problems of factory hands and quarrelsome young husbands and wives. Studies of middle-class individuals, although such individuals abound in modern society, are hopelessly out of date.

It was not so in the new fashions of the nineteen-twenties, when only the 'first-class' was valued. Bloomsbury, confident in its own modernity and superiority, swept into temporary power. Its leaders had assembled during the War at the Morrells' home near Oxford, where poets and intellectuals found warm hospitality; and they seemed to take possession of the critical journals, in which they propagated their Faith. Even *The Athenaeum*, to the editorship of which John Middleton Murry succeeded, was so much in thrall that I, never an intellectual, had a pathetic appeal for contributions from Murry. He wanted defences against the new power.

I recently came across a letter of Murry's to myself which began 'I enjoyed my lunch with you very much indeed; it's such a pleasure to talk with someone who isn't superior or dishonest, and it helped a great deal to pull me out of a general depression about things in general and literature in particular.'

I draw attention to these words 'superior and dishonest'. Murry has been condemned for his apparent willingness to cash in on Katherine Mansfield's posthumous reputation; but at the time this letter was written (it is dated only 'Wednesday', and must belong to 1919) K.M. was still alive, and they were working together in a steady partnership.

The Athenaeum and *The Nation*, which latter had been brilliantly edited by H. W. Massingham, were swept away in due course, in spite of *The Athenaeum's* regular contributions from Katherine Mansfield and Aldous Huxley. The *English Review*, under J. C. Squire, who had his own band of brotherly regulars, foundered. They were not sufficiently *avant garde*. We all had been told that the only novelists worth reading were Virginia Woolf, D. H. Lawrence, and James Joyce; and the only poets and critics the metaphysicians.

Bennett, who represented 'the plain man', had other vexations, including the appearance as a serial in *The Daily Express* of Marguerite's self-justifying book, *My Arnold Bennett*. Beaverbrook saw no harm in this effort; but Bennett, fearing that the public would suppose he had authorized it as a piece of publicity, was dismayed. He was worried by his increased weight and the sense that he was now visibly middle-aged. He had an impression that his day had passed, and that, with all his fame and all his responsibilities, he might find himself back in the poverty of his youth. If asked how he was, he would sometimes answer 'I . . . am gloomy'.

There was another element. His disappointments and embarrassments were accompanied by new personal hostilities to himself, which he endured without retaliation. Although in every respect liberal, he had become in many eyes, as a result of his appointment to the Ministry of Information under Churchill, a professional Tory politician. His company was sought by Party Leaders. It was suggested that ambition had carried him out of his proper sphere into a world he had longed to enter. And, finally, Lady Rhondda chose to believe that *Lord Raingo* was an attack on her father's memory. She therefore said melodramatically to some friends of mine, the St John Ervines, 'I'll *break* that man!'

I do not know how Lady Rhondda proposed to break Bennett, and she is now dead. Her assumption that *Lord Raingo* was a book about her father was quite unwarranted. It was about Arnold Bennett, his experience at the Ministry of Information, and Dorothy Cheston. Details of Cabinet

Meetings came from Beaverbrook; but in essence the book is a highly personal document. Lady Rhondda's hatred of the author was one of the political animosities of the time. It was undeserved. Bennett, in company for a weekend at Beaverbrook's with two of the most celebrated political leaders of the day, discovered from their conversation that they were more concerned with the ruin of their opponents than with the good of the country. In the natural simplicity and kindness of his heart he had never imagined such cynicism to be possible. Wishing to be thought unshockable, he made no comment to others; but to myself he confided that he had been horrified.

The *Evening Standard* articles constituted a set-back to the partisans of Bloomsbury. The articles were extraordinarily successful and influential. In their first year, at least, they boosted several books into wide sales, and made a number of new reputations. But they naturally displeased the cliques and the purists. One highly intellectual man of my acquaintance fulminated against them, concluding his remarks with the hysterical cry 'The trouble is, he's always so damned interesting!'

The articles were interesting because Bennett himself had an insatiable interest in phenomena. He noticed all sorts of things as he walked along the streets, from women's dresses in the shop windows to the behaviour of shop assistants. At that time an ingenious firm of clothes-repairers hit on the notion of picturing young seamstresses at work in their shop windows, and he wrote an article on the theme which his editor (not himself) billed as 'Decent Exposure'. He continued to read Dostoevsky, whom he had introduced to the British public before Mrs Garnett translated the complete works; but he also re-read Gibbon and kept up a running acquaintance with the work of newcomers to the literary world. On one occasion I remember his saying as we walked together along Regent Street 'I've been reading Shelley. There's something *in* him.' It was a discovery. The man who long before had written a manual on *Literary Taste: how to Form it* was reading to learn all the time, and to announce his acquisition of new knowledge. He did this, about books, week after week, with the abruptness of a stammerer and the unsophisticated delight of a young traveller in 'the realms of gold' and copper. Nothing came amiss.

Sir Stanley Unwin always claimed that it was he who suggested to Beaverbrook the employment of Bennett as literary critic. If so, he showed once again the wonderful instinct for publishing which led him to jump at Lancelot Hogben's *Mathematics for the Million* after it had been rejected as too long by an enterprising rival. Bennett was to write for *The Evening Standard*, at a large fee (I think it was a hundred pounds a week, but reports increased that sum) the sort of thing 'Jacob Tonson' had written, gratuitously, for *The New Age* in 1908–11. But his situation was different. He could not speak, in 1926, under his own name, as cheekily as he had done, under a pseudonym, in his youth. He remained 'the plain man', interested, not in a school, but in every aspect of life and letters. And he believed it to be his duty to review new and sometimes inferior books in a manner fair to all.

In this connection I hope I shall not be thought intrusive if I say that when, in 1929, I was invited to write superficially comparable articles for the London *Evening News*, it was mutually agreed that, as friends, we should not review each other's books. This was characteristic of Bennett, whose example I followed until my Editor, fearing that he would be accused of crabbing his rival's star reviewer, asked me to notice *Imperial Palace*. I did this, reluctantly, and Bennett was not altogether satisfied with what I said.

In spite of the fact that we were very widely read by literary people, we were both labelled 'commercial'; and Bennett, because he went on pouring out novels and short stories and articles, was repeatedly charged with doing this for love of money. As I have already said, he suffered from an ingrained habit of industry. As soon as he woke up in the morning, unless he had done so during a sleepless night, he reached for his pen. This was never the case with myself. I am a ruminant, and have always worked with reluctance. Bennett found this quite perverse.

Once, after spending five days in every week reading other men's typescripts, and my evenings and weekends in composing and finishing a book, I had a week or so on the *Marie Marguerite*. Excusably, I thought, I basked on deck in the summer sunshine, hands clasped in complete relaxation. Bennett stood this for two days, but on the third he said sharply 'I say, you're not *writing* anything.' I said 'No, I'm on a holiday.' He retorted 'But you're not *reading* anything, either.' I, still thankful at a lucky escape from typescripts, said 'No. I'm on a holiday.' He, outraged, charged me with being 'idle' (his most condemnatory word): and when I reminded him that I had always confessed to temperamental idleness, he said with great severity 'Yes, I know. But it's *true*!'

I was cast into utter darkness for five minutes.

Arnold Bennett
Inscribed 'to Henry', his nickname for F.S.

Marguerite Bennett
Inscribed to F.S.

A.B. the baseline tennis player (with Marguerite)

Dorothy Cheston Bennett

Family group at Paris-Plage. (Virginia, Nurse, Mary S., A.B. and F.S.)

A.B. nursing Virginia

John Galsworthy holding Virginia

F.S. idling

10

Although using his own yacht, the *Marie Marguerite*, upon which the conversation just recorded took place, Bennett often spent short periods on other yachts, including *Amaryllis*, owned by Herbert Sullivan, the nephew of Sir Arthur. This was a smaller craft than his own (I once had a cramped week-end upon it near Ipswich, during which I caught the cold of a lifetime); but she was able to cruise along the French and Belgian coasts and as far south as the Mediterranean when Sullivan could get an engineer who knew his job. Bennett wrote from Monte Carlo to Winifred Nerney, sending to be typed 22,000 words of *Lilian* which he had written while on 'holiday', and giving her instructions about home affairs.

'Re Rose', he said, in the course of his long letter, 'I don't like my maids to be dressed in black, and I want her to look much smarter than she does herself. I will give her a dark blue or a light blue or some other colour costume and aprons and caps to match, to start her. But it will of course be necessary for you to check and get these things from a good shop, and they must be the latest thing. I have seen many good ones in the West End and I see no reason why a maid should not be encouraged to make the best of herself. I hope to God you have cured her of saying "Thank you" in reply to an order.'

The reference to 22,000 words of *Lilian* explains why he was so shocked by my idleness aboard the *Marie Marguerite*; and it says much for his terrible industry that Bennett had written a third of this short novel while doing 'a tremendous lot of dancing—with both professionals and amateurs' and meeting and being entertained by other yachtsmen or visitors to Cannes and Monte Carlo. One new acquaintance he made in the latter place was the Baroness Orczy, author of *The Scarlet Pimpernel*, 'a very decent Jewess, enormous.' And he was convinced that his dancing alone saved him from being seriously ill—a danger never far from his mind.

This was no more than one aspect of his life after Marguerite left the flat in George Street. His acquaintance extended to members of the young Smart Set, who aroused the puritanism in his nature. Of one female set in particular I remember him saying grimly 'They're all impure. They've all been seduced.' But others did divert him, and he enjoyed their company. These were his 'children', who ranged from Harriet Cohen and Dorothy Cheston to a married couple named Godebski. He was punctilious in his regard for propriety; and on one occasion he wrote to Winifred, saying 'I wired you today to come over here (Ostend) on Saturday, by the first service if poss . . . I should like to go into a number of things with you. . . . One of my most powerful reasons for asking you to come is that those two women here, Mrs Roberts and Miss Cheston, have made a muddle of their stay between them. They particularly wanted to stay till Monday, July 30th (1923). Now Mrs Roberts has to leave on Saturday, and Miss Cheston can't leave till Monday at earliest as her house is closed till then. I've no intention of having Miss Cheston here alone with Percy Jowett and me. The social conventions have to be observed in this yacht, and so I thought that by getting you I should kill two birds with one stone. The weather is *not* good, though bright. Mr Sullivan has started out twice to get to Boulogne and has had to return owing to bad weather. Each time he went contrary to advice, and so he is the more furious.'

Presumably Winifred went, and returned to London in due course, for she wrote to Bennett on August 13, saying 'I note that you will want me to come aboard at the end of the month. Have you any idea of the date you will want me to come, as I should like to leave everything ready here for your return.' She concluded her letter with some motherly advice. 'It is an awful nuisance about your insomnia. The only thing I can suggest is a good sharp walk after dinner at night and a cup of Ovaltine just before you go to bed, but I'm afraid perhaps it isn't a very practical suggestion. Ovaltine is recommended by most specialists now for sleeplessness. Something will obviously have to be done to cure it.'

'Something will obviously have to be done to cure it.' Those words must have caused Bennett to smile. He had consulted various specialists about his stammer, to no avail; he must have had constant advice from his friend Dr Shufflebotham, who urged dancing as a means of losing weight, about his insomnia. Stammer and insomnia lasted until the end of his life.

What is interesting in these extracts, besides the candour of his statements to Winifred (they remained to the last 'Mr Bennett' and 'Miss Nerney') is the fact that he was strictly 'observing the conventions' with Dorothy. I have already said that she was a dazzling blonde; and by her own account it would seem that she had a schoolgirlish innocence of the world's ways when they first met. In fact she was over thirty at that time, had been on the stage for a number of years in both America and England. She had toured in, among other plays, Sadermann's *Magda*, and was well able to look after herself. Moreover her eager behaviour towards Bennett had been so marked in Liverpool that it led Arthur Bouchier to tell her, with cynical roguery, that Bennett's marriage had broken down. What thoughts roamed in that beautiful head it is impossible to say; but if I describe Dorothy as 'a child of Nature' I shall give a clue, I hope, to some characteristics which will be illustrated in later pages. Bennett was not a pursuer of women. He had demanded Duff Tayler's close presence at their departure from Liverpool because '*she* is coming to see us off.' I think that Dorothy had not only achieved a new male friendship, but formed a resolution.

What more natural? She was ambitious for a stage career; she had been told by Mrs Patrick Campbell that she was worth encouraging; she saw in Bennett one who not only wrote plays but could influence theatrical Managers. It must have seemed a heaven-sent opportunity. There comes a tide in the affairs of Women that, taken at the flood, leads on to fortune. The tide was rising.

In the rather confused narrative of her relations with Bennett forming part of *A Portrait Done at Home*, Dorothy implies that the advances to intimacy were made by Bennett. His invitations to tea or dinner are printed; but none of her own correspondence. This is not necessarily disingenuous; but she was an extraordinarily copious letter writer, as is shown by her letters to me. In one instance I received a communication running to twenty large pages; and if she wasted such length upon a minor friend she was probably still more verbose in writing to somebody of much greater consequence to her. Bennett was evidently impressed by her labours.

He did, furthermore, commend her to several theatrical Managers, to Dennis Eadie, to Frederick Harrison, and finally, with success, to Donald Calthrop, who was producing *As You Like It*. She also had a small part in a revival of *The Great Adventure*. Their friendship, beginning with dances and piano duets, which he loved to play, grew more intimate. She was full of energy; she stimulated him; he introduced her to his friends, by whom she was accepted as 'Arnold's girl friend'.

I was out of England for five months in the Winter of 1923–4, at first on a tour of the United States, and afterwards on honeymoon in Italy. Therefore I saw comparatively little of Bennett while the love affair was maturing. On my return from Italy I was asked by him to consult Sir John Withers, the Solicitor, whom I had met previously, on the possibility of a divorce from Marguerite. This was really out of the question, because Marguerite had previously refused such a total break; and Sir John, having listened to what I had to report, merely shook his head in dismissal of the idea.

Other elements contributed to what was seen as an impossibility. One was Bennett's inability to articulate when under stress, which would make torture of any appearance in a witness box. Another was worldwide and perhaps vicious publicity. And in those days there was not, as there is now, a clause in the law whereby non-cohabitation for a certain period is sufficient ground for divorce by either party. My errand was fruitless.

In the summer of 1925 came a further problem. Bennett and I, lunching with others at our Club, met for a brief chat before lunch. This was in the great entrance hall of the Reform. Suddenly he said, at his most abrupt, 'Dorothy's going to . . . have a child.' He spoke as if the event was an accident which might happen to anybody; but it was clear that he was considerably disturbed. He was foreseeing the inevitable sequels, which included the reorganization of his now settled way of life.

No discussion of those sequels took place between us. He assumed that, as he was doing, I should perceive all consequences. For one thing, he must be an efficient father. Therefore he must abandon all bachelor habits. The *Marie Marguerite* must go; Winifred Nerney and his affectionate staff must be protected from anxiety and unhappiness; everything must be orderly and responsible. As Winifred was on holiday, he wrote to her on September 1st, 1925, in these terms:

'Dear Miss Nerney, I have never mentioned to you the subject of my relations with Dorothy Cheston, because I felt that if I did so, formally, I might put you in a rather delicate position. I thought it was better that you should have no formal knowledge of them from me; and my reserve was in no way due to any lack of confidence in your discretion and your loyalty, which to my mind have always been unsurpassable and for which I could not be too grateful. Happily Miss Cheston has been received by my principal friends exactly as if she were my wife, which she ought to be and would be if circumstances permitted, but on the other hand we have observed all the external conventions. The situation is now going to be complicated by the fact there is a strong possibility of Miss Cheston becoming a mother. I tell you this because I prefer to be open with you in so important a matter, and not because it will make any difference at all to the external conventions of my life here (75 Cadogan Square). I detest concealing things from you, as I think you have deserved better from me than that. I shall take Miss Cheston away for a time towards the end of the year. In the meantime, and afterwards, things will go on precisely as usual so far as you and this house are concerned.

Yours sincerely, ARNOLD BENNETT.

11

True to his nature, Bennett recollected all that he had learned as a young man while working, first as sub-editor, and then as editor, on a weekly journal called *Woman*. He was familiar with the details of layettes; he superintended the choice of a maternity home and the installation of Dorothy in that maternity home; and although his distaste for the atmosphere of sick rooms was famous, he visited her before and after the birth of their daughter, Virginia Mary. His preoccupation with the whole process of introducing a new life to the world was intense.

He was also hounded by a sense that Dorothy and the baby would suffer personal disadvantage because he could not end his marriage with Marguerite. It never did end until his death; and even then Marguerite, convinced that he would send for her, hovered near, waiting for the summons. She absolutely refused to let another woman take her place as Mrs Arnold Bennett.

In the dilemma Bennett resolved at last that Dorothy should take the name of Bennett by Deed Poll; and thenceforward she was to be known as Mrs Dorothy Cheston Bennett. It followed that she and their daughter must live at 75 Cadogan Square under his care and with the service of the existing staff, headed, naturally, by Winifred Nerney. It is from conversations with Winifred Nerney that I have gathered facts about what happened in the house.

Mrs Anita Miller, who knows by study of Bennett's work and *Journals* more than anybody alive, except perhaps James Hepburn, about his temperament and performance, suggests that the servants at Cadogan Square took a high moral line at the introduction there of a mistress and her child. They may have disapproved; but I think their love and respect for

Bennett, as well as Virginia's charm, which was generally acknowledged, would have smoothed everything if other circumstances has been different. These were circumstances of personality.

Dorothy had never before been in charge of a considerable establishment. She was used to bed-sitters and, as a touring actress, provincial lodgings. She was also impatient and sure that she was right. Her energy was so great that she would seize a man by his coat lapels and shake him in order to emphasize the point she wanted to make. She did this with me. Her teeth clenched; her greenish eyes became as fixed as those of a mesmerist or a sleepwalker. Nothing must stand in the way of whatever she had determined.

Now in the early months of acquaintance, when they were meeting only at intervals, this energy was obviously attractive to Bennett. It fitted in with his Victorian, almost Barrie-like, belief that young women were irresponsible children who had to be humoured. He had learned from the young sophisticates (who figured thenceforward in his plays and such tales as *The Woman who Stole Everything*) that their irresponsibility might become immorality, which he condemned; but in Dorothy's case the energy, the earnestness, the pertinacity of her demands for his attention amused until they overwhelmed him. Amusement, even marvel, is testified in his letters to her. She says in the *Portrait Done at Home*, quite credibly, that he kissed her as they sat together after playing a piano duet, and that on another occasion he took her hand, saying 'I'm in love with you, you see.'

Not everything Dorothy said, in conversation or in print, was true; it was what she *wanted* to believe, and invented for personal satisfaction. Therefore the kiss did not necessarily occur, and this speech, like others she reported, may not have been made. But I think Bennett was really in love with her, and protectively resolved to maintain her good name. This accounts for his concern with what he called 'the external conventions', which in the affairs of another man would have seemed to him unimportant. In the same way he took very seriously his responsibility towards the coming baby. As he had so often said before, of others, 'She had to be helped'. In other words, she must be directly under his care, and supported by acknowledged paternity. This could only be effected if both Dorothy and the child came to live at 75 Cadogan Square.

Robert Louis Stevenson wrote 'To marry is to domesticate the Recording Angel'; and while, until she wrote *A Portrait Done at Home*, Dorothy was no Recording Angel, she was unquestionably a disruptive force in an orderly home. Everything there had hitherto been governed as if by stop watch. Order, punctuality, politeness, and, above all, quiet were necessary to a man who began working before breakfast, and continued with little interruption throughout the day. As to the night, Bennett thought he had done well if he slept for three hours, free from terrible pains in the head which always followed exhaustion or over-excitement.

It is a proof of his simplicity that he imagined Dorothy capable of taking her place in a time-tabled establishment, and even contributing to its comfort, while her position remained ambiguous. The contrary was soon proved. The servants had been used to requests from a man whose courtesy to all was exemplary. They neither felt nor pretended any respect for an interloper who, tasting power, issued commands.

There was a further difficulty. The name adopted by Deed Poll, 'Dorothy Cheston Bennett', was not always used. Winifred Nerney, still in correspondence with Marguerite, whom she had offered to help, was told that bills for goods ordered in the name of 'Mrs Arnold Bennett' were being sent, not to Dorothy, but to the real Mrs Bennett. Winifred was asked by Marguerite to clear the situation. She did her best. She also tried to deal with indignant servants. Finally she had to deal with Dorothy.

I do not know how she managed to do all these things, for she was typing Bennett's books and articles and short stories, writing a great many business letters on his behalf, keeping his accounts, and ascertaining just what items should be included in his Income Tax returns and what claims should be made under the head of 'expenses'. In the midst of this devoted secretarial work, she told me, she would hear screams and discover that Dorothy, in a paroxysm of rage, had thrown herself face downward on the stairs and was beating them with her clenched fists. 75 Cadogan Square, formerly sedate, had become a storm centre.

As late as 1929 Bennett could write to Dorothy, with

humour, that he was gloomy without her 'exciting presence'. The exciting presence was occasionally withdrawn when Dorothy went abroad or to Brighton or elsewhere on some short theatrical tour. Her absorption in the theatre, although she was never a successful actress, was considerable, and from time to time she managed to pick up a part. Except for one assignment, Viola in the quickly extinguished production of *As You Like It*, the part was usually a small one. She also, on the assumption that Bennett's income would always meet every need, experimented with productions of her own, which lost money. At one time she revived *Milestones*, the play in which Bennett collaborated with Edward Knoblock; and after one rehearsal I remember her return home with a triumphant claim that 'we're getting *pace* on it!' But the increased pace was unavailing. The production was a failure. Another effort, a dramatized version of *Mr Prohack*, with Charles Laughton giving an impersonation of Bennett in the principal part, was soon withdrawn: and Bennett himself reminded her in 1930 that 'you will never in the end make money by play-producing on your own.' Dorothy thought she could do so; and the losses were met out of his literary earnings. With two thousand pounds a year guaranteed to Marguerite, and those losses, he was justified in his rueful comment to me: 'Women are great gold-drinkers.'

When Dorothy was away, he wrote to her; but when play-producing was in hand she was at home. She then thought nothing of interrupting his work or keeping him up at night for the discussion of her theatrical projects, which soon included a translation into English and production in London and New York of Bourdet's play *Vient de Paraitre*. Bennett was similarly interrupted, according to Winifred Nerney, in order that he might adjust domestic matters which had reached a point of what is nowadays called 'confrontation'. Only he, it appeared, could calm the antagonists. For some time he could perhaps have used a favourite phrase 'And I did do'; but the task grew more formidable week by week.

Nothing of all this was mentioned to his men friends. Pride forbade. Pride, not only in Arnold Bennett, the imperturbable, but in all Staffordshire men. 'We are of the North', he wrote in his *Journal* in 1896, 'outwardly brusque, stoical, undemonstrative, scornful of the impulsive; inwardly all sentiment and crushed tenderness.' I cannot confirm the generalization, but the words certainly applied to Arnold Bennett. His men friends did not see the crushed tenderness. They were conscious of his outflowing kindness; but they never heard from him the smallest confession of weakness.

It is just possible that he related some of his distresses to Pauline Smith, the South African writer of Scottish descent, whose book *The Little Karoo* contains some of the most poignant stories ever written in English. She was a most sensitive and understanding woman, to whom he wrote quite regularly, on condition that his letters were destroyed as soon as she had read them; and in its place I shall record an incident which showed the view she held of Dorothy. When I first saw her, in 1916, she was still young; but she gave the impression, sitting with her hands folded and with a knitted shawl round her shoulders, of being an old granny. She spoke, moreover, almost inaudibly, in a hushed voice. Very sweet, I thought; but very old.

She was not at all old. She was probably not much over thirty. And as I came to know her really well I saw the folly of my first judgment. She had great humour and immense courage, whether it involved keeping absolutely still in South Africa while a huge malignant green snake crawled around and over her, or climbing into an upstairs window of the house she shared with her sister in Broadstone, Dorset, because she had forgotten her doorkey. When she visited us my daughter, then very young, instantly went to stand close to her; an admirer to whom I introduced her said she was the most impressive personality he had ever met. And, as I can testify, her wisdom was profound.

It is possible, as I say, that Bennett told Pauline what he never, for example, told me. My own opinion was formed as a result of direct observation, contacts, and, later, communications from Winifred Nerney, Bennett's sister Tertia, and his daughter Virginia. Winifred Nerney testified to his patience; and Dorothy told me herself that, although she makes no mention of the fact in her book about Bennett, the pavement outside 75 Cadogan Square was chalked with offensive remarks about her which must, one assumes, have been scrawled there by some discharged and indignant servant. The 'external conventions' having been flouted, a penalty was being paid.

12

A closer association with Dorothy began for myself after the birth of Virginia Mary Bennett. Bennett wished to establish a Trust Fund for her; and as for legal reasons he could not be one of the Trustees himself he asked me to share this responsibility with Dorothy. I shall give certain details regarding the Trust in a later chapter; but as I have just indicated some of the strains arising in the Bennett household I think it only right at this point to say that although we sometimes disagreed, and I found her interferences and many-paged letters rather tiresome, Dorothy and I never once quarrelled.

In the Summer of 1928 the Bennetts rented a house at Le Touquet; and as my wife and I were at Etaples, Bennett, perhaps remembering with pleasure our visit to Portugal, suggested that we should remove to Paris-Plage, which was, as it were, next door to them. We met almost every day, he and I strolling, the whole party sitting on the sands, or Dorothy and my wife bathing. The Bennetts had a bathing hut, and Virginia (for my wife and I had not yet started a family) was the star attraction. All went well.

All went well, that is, until Dorothy, a great sightseer, decided that it would be entertaining to visit Amiens. They had their car; we hired a local car; and as our driver knew the way my wife and I set off in the lead. We had not gone very far, however, before we were summoned to stop. Our car was no flier, and besides slowing up the progress it was emitting fumes that made Dorothy feel unwell. Would we mind if the Bennett car went first? We did not mind. If they went far enough ahead we should not be in the way and there would be no fumes. After all, we were out for a day's pleasure.

Abbeville was reached. The two young women went off on a tour of the town while Bennett and I made a leisurely examination of the nearer streets. In the course of this examination we came to an hotel and restaurant which exhibited its menu for that day's *dejeuner*. Bennett scrutinized this menu with deep interest, giving each item his full attention, and coming to a favourable conclusion as to the whole meal, 'This . . . looks very good', he said. 'We might lunch here, don't you think?' I agreed that the place and meal were both attractive, and supposed the matter settled. But when Dorothy came racing back, and he said to her 'We . . . thought we might lunch here', she vehemently cried 'No, no! We *must* get on to Amiens!' There was no inquiry as to what the others would like; we simply replaced ourselves in the two cars, with ours bringing up the rear as before.

Amiens was reached rather late, I think about half-past two; but we quickly found a restaurant which, in true French fashion, made arrangements to feed the party. There were several brusqueries during the meal; and I must admit that, although temperamentally patient, I grew tired of behaviour which implied that in spite of bearing our full share of the expense, plus the hired car, my wife and I were Dorothy's poor relations.

Finally it came, as I supposed, to the moment for our return journey. But that was not Dorothy's view. She imperiously cried 'No, no! We *must* see the Puvis de Chavannes collection!' Bennett stood silent. He had been silent most of the time. It was for me to act. I said, laughingly, 'Oh, Puvis de Chavannes is quite *démodé*. Ever since people discovered Piero della Francesca!' Dorothy's determination collapsed. She had never heard of Piero della Francesca; and the word *démodé* had made it seem that she was pursuing a Victorian freak. All wish to see the Puvis de Chavannes collection faded. Bennett gave me a long searching look, completely free from disapproval. We at once began our journey back to the coast.

I tell this story because it illustrates two things. The first is that Bennett, who was terribly concerned at the thought that when Virginia was ten years old he would be seventy, no longer had the power to resist a wilful woman. He was by no means at the end of his genius and his writing capacity; but the sense of Dorothy's vigour, which he still believed the sign of an intelligence and originality which was not apparent to his family and his friends, was reminding him that he was more than twenty years her senior. The second is that Dorothy's self-assurance, however much it might force Bennett into silent acquiescence, was really superficial. I used to know a very pleasant woman of middle age who boasted that she had been to prison as a Suffragette; and this woman's slogan was 'I go on until I'm stopped; and I find that I never am stopped.' A young woman with Dorothy's looks and drive could insist on doing what she wanted to do, as long as her intelligence was believed in. In the face of irreverence she had neither the wit nor the humour to retort. She then revealed the intellectual (not moral) innocence of a child.

To complete the story of our stay at Paris-Plage, I shall mention that Bennett one morning asked us to dine with them. I was parting with Dorothy before lunch, and said 'You'll be seeing us later. Arnold has asked us to dinner.' Her reply was 'Oh, no; you can't come. We're going out.' I thought this conflict between the two rather strange; but was not at all offended. What did cause me considerable indignation was that on the last day of our stay, when we really had been asked to dinner by both Dorothy and Bennett, she was guilty of unjustified rudeness to my wife. The two women had agreed to bathe in the afternoon. My wife was punctual but was kept waiting for ten minutes. At last Dorothy came flying across the sands, dashed without greeting into the bathing hut, and slammed the door in my wife's face.

Arriving shortly afterwards, I found my wife in great distress. Her natural gentleness provided no answer to such behaviour. Knowing this, and resentful on her behalf, I wrote Dorothy a polite note at teatime explaining that, with regret, we could not dine after all, as we had to pack that evening for departure very early in the morning. We then ordered dinner in the hotel, and were eating it when Bennett arrived. He had set out, on hearing of my note, with the intention of persuading us to change our minds; but he was deeply disturbed, and said 'I've been looking forward to it all day.' Although no complaint had been made, he must have guessed the cause of my note. Much against our inclination we agreed to meet the two for a drink later that night, and at this meeting we noticed that Dorothy, though full of charm, said not a word.

After Bennett's death she wrote to me complaining that Arnold's friends had deserted her, and asking if I could suggest any reason. I ventured the possible explanation that she might sometimes have been rather brusque with them. She was extremely pained, and assured me that she had never in her life been brusque with anybody. It was not in her nature to be so. This is what I meant when I referred to her innocence.

13

It may not have been noticed by casual readers, but I think it is significant, that while Bennett himself published a heavily cut version of his *Journal* for 1929, the edition of the *Journal* edited in three volumes by Newman Flower produced in 1932–3 comes to a stop on December 31st, 1928. Also that the letters quoted in Dorothy's *Portrait Done at Home* thin out considerably in later months, and after August, 1929 there are only a dozen for 1930, of which eight were written while Bennett was on a yachting excursion with A. E. W. Mason, the last of them dated six months before Bennett's death. What happened between the Bennetts in 1930 and the first months of 1931 is nowhere suggested.

I do not know why there should have been any suppression of the *Journal*; but if it has taken place the reason can be guessed. The relationship between the two must have become extremely difficult. Bennett had already given a warning, in letters printed in *A Portrait Done at Home* that the losses on Dorothy's theatrical ventures were greater than his resources would allow. 'I really ought not to tie up money in this way'; 'don't deceive yourself about play-producing as a livelihood'; 'As regards finance, I don't know that I am gloomy. I don't see that it is gloomy to state the facts. I say really very little about it. But whether much or little is said about it, *it is there.*'

Money trouble was not the only trouble. Bennett was still making a good deal of money, not in the theatre, but by his books and by journalism. He had been writing political articles for various periodicals and his regular weekly *causerie* in *The Evening Standard* was (to the rage of all highbrows) paid for at top rates. He was not, therefore, in want, nor, in normal circumstances, could he have feared a financial collapse. What was really dangerous was his effort to keep up with Dorothy's absorption in the theatre, the exhaustingness of supporting her zest for theatrical and other society, and, worst of all, the lack of rest. His insomnia was more severe than ever. He was made to stay up, and to keep awake, while Dorothy loaded him with details of her plans. Even his work was interrupted, and sometimes made impossible, by endless talk of the theatre.

As an example of the exhaustingness of theatrical life, here is an extract from the *Journal* for 1929. In it he describes one visit to Portsmouth for the first performance of a play 'prior to London production' at the Theatre Royal there. 'There isn't a theatre in the West End, except Covent Garden, to compare with it. The cast was pure West End. But Portsmouth audiences are not to be intimidated. They are constantly seeing genuine West End productions. At the rival theatre (no, not the rival, because both theatres are under one proprietorship) a first-class London star was "opening" on that self-same night with a new play. The hotel was markedly theatrical. After the performance groups of actors, actresses and playwrights supped endlessly in its dining-room, whose waiters are accustomed to late hours. I talked with various artists.

'The talk was solely, endlessly, of the stage. I doubt whether actors and actresses ever talk about anything but the stage. I am quite sure they never tire of the subject. As an inexhaustible subject the stage beats hunting, golf and fishing hollow. At a few minutes to 1 a.m. I bade goodnight. Everybody seemed surprised that I should retire so early. Everybody was still eating and drinking and talking eagerly, and without the least sign of fatigue, about the stage. And the waiters were still quite lively. The night-porter told me how stars, whom he named by name, would stay up talking till 5 a.m. He thought nothing of that. Actors and actresses must have the physique of explorers.'

Dorothy was one of the actresses. She had the physique, and the determination, of a mountain-climber, and the rapid talkativeness of a chatterbox. She could stay up until the night was far spent, in unceasing monologue about the stage and her schemes for the stage. Bennett, without the physique of either actor or explorer, was sixty-two, and when he went to bed he could not rest. Neuralgia tormented him. And, somehow, he had to continue to work hard at writing which called for the utmost mental and imaginative concentration.

I have already spoken of the need for pacifying indignant or rebellious staff, and of the chalked abuse of Dorothy on the pavement outside 75 Cadogan Square. The pacification wearied him and he was much agitated by the abuse. And the calls on his time and purse were endless. He was regarded as patron and friend by those he never saw (one letter he showed me began 'Dear Mr Bennett, I think *The Old Wives' Tale* is the finest novel I ever read. And now I want to tell you about my trouble.' It was a request for cash. I said 'A bit thick!' and he answered 'I get them all the time.'). He was now more and more feeling his years; and the monetary situation 'appalled' him.

Still more serious was the fact that Dorothy grew more imperious than ever. Quarrels between them became, on her side, stormy, and, on his, silently obdurate. She later, in writing to me, said that much disagreements arose from rigidities in Arnold's character. This, as my old employer J. M. Dent would have said, was 'a misnomer'. The conflict was between an irresistible force and an immovable object, between Dorothy's wild and ever-increasing egocentricity and Bennett's loving but obstinate determination not to be overwhelmed by a termagant.

His humour remained alive, even when Dorothy sought to dictate the kind of book he should write; but her instructions may well have been galling to a highly individual artist of unsurpassed experience. During earlier years in the United States she had known John Cowper Powys, a good critic as well as writer of enormous and in my opinion over-portentous novels; and she had learnt from Powys, at least superficially, certain literary canons. Having no humour, and being a sort of synthetic highbrow, she saw herself as an inspired judge. The persuasion was not continuous; she could lose confidence in herself; but when active it led to domestic assertiveness. And no author likes to have a literary critic on the hearth. What he needs there is moral support against detractors abroad. Dorothy gave Bennett no such support.

She, too, had by this time become an author. That is to say, she had translated the Bourdet play and was bent on achieving both fame and fortune through this play. Her work on it had begun before we spent our holiday at Paris-Plage, and I there read some of the translation, which I thought smelled of the dictionary. Later, she went to Paris to interview the author, and her expectations from it were incredible. They continued so from month to month, long after Bennett's death.

When the inevitable removal from Cadogan Square took place the Bennetts went to live in an impressive block of flats over Baker Street railway station, perhaps because H. G. Wells was already in residence there. Wells's flat was on an upper floor, and was of normal size. That in which the Bennetts proposed to live was too small for their needs, and to accommodate them two flats were converted into one. My memory of it is of a long corridor with a series of doors on both sides of it, such as one finds in a large hotel. No doubt this fact would have delighted those who pictured Bennett as enraptured by the grandiose; but I think the explanation of its size was simply that with a baby, a nurse, a secretary, and the need for a workroom for Bennett, besides dining-room, drawing-room, and bedrooms for everybody, quite an extensive place was needed. The rooms were not excessively large; and there cannot have been enough of them, because Dorothy, as a literary woman, once appropriated Bennett's study for her own use.

This probably did not happen a second time; but it will be realized that his discovery that somebody was sitting in his chair caused temporary consternation. Unfortunately, this act of piracy was an indication that disagreements had passed from petty quarrels to crises. On her first night in the flat, as she told my wife and myself, Dorothy found the vibration caused by Underground trains below intolerable. The memorable phrase she used was 'It went right up my rectum.' Bennett, greatly troubled, toiled up to Wells's flat two floors above, and asked Wells if she might sleep there on the following night. Wells demurred, saying 'You know my reputation, Arnold', to which Bennett grimly replied 'I'll risk it.' This was related to me by Wells himself.

Winifred Nerney added other details, which included a

decision on Bennett's part that this state of affairs could not continue. Dorothy countered with a stipulation that if they separated she must have exactly what Marguerite had, namely two thousand pounds a year. This would be in addition to the income derived from Virginia's Trust Fund, of which the capital amount was thirteen thousand pounds, and the value of manuscripts and copyrights already transferred to her in happier days. During a lull in hostilities, they agreed to go to France together, to see Bourdet and to stay with Jo Davidson, the American sculptor, at his lovely Manoir near Tours. But the lull was seen by Bennett without illusion. He had reached a decision. Before they left he said ominously to Winifred Nerney 'I shall bring back a very different woman—or else . . .'

14

While I was writing the weekly book article for *The Evening News*, which appeared on Fridays, it was my habit to go to London on the Friday, chiefly in order to see my editor, Frank FitzHugh, in the afternoon. I normally went to the Reform Club before lunch, and saw Bennett sitting in the big entrance hall. He had walked from Cadogan Square, and had read my article that morning. Only if I had made some grammatical mistake did he refer to the article.

Very often we joined a delightful circle of men of whom I think to this day with affection and gratitude. The dominating member was an astonishingly nimble ex-MP named Walter Roch, whose fun and impudent teasing kept all the others alert; but other 'regulars' included judges, scholars, magistrates, Harold McKenna (Bow Street) and Walter Hedley (Marlborough Street), ex-editors or editors A. G. Gardiner, J. A. Spender, and H. W. Massingham, a sprinkling of politicians who ranged from Sir John Tudor Walters and Lord Rhayader (formerly Leif Jones) to Vivian Phillipps, the chief Liberal whip. Sometimes H. G. Wells would join us. The talk was the best I ever heard. Bennett spoke little, unless appealed to for an opinion; but he always added his own benignity to the proceedings, and was loved by all.

On the 23rd of January, 1931, I did not go to the Reform Club, because I was meeting George Doran, the American publisher, for lunch at the Savoy Hotel. A few days before then I received a note from Bennett saying that he particularly wanted to talk to me: could I meet him on the 23rd? In reply, I said I was engaged to Doran, and suggested that he should invite himself to the party. Alternatively, I would come up specially on any day he liked.

Bennett sent a further note, explaining that he wanted to

see me alone, that he would not steal one of my working days, and that my usual day in the following week would do quite well. But before the following Friday I had word from Winifred Nerney that Bennett had returned from France with influenza, and could not keep our appointment. During the next few days several communications passed between Winifred and myself, sometimes by letter, sometimes by telephone. I learned that Bennett's illness, at first diagnosed as influenza, had proved to be paratyphoid fever, that the doctor had forbidden visitors, but that Bennett had been told of my concern, for which he was grateful. The illness was soon afterwards recognized to be real typhoid.

It was said that he had insisted upon drinking carafe water in a Paris restaurant, and Jo Davidson, remembering that his guest had drunk water at Becheron, was in a state of distress lest the poison should have been absorbed there. Dorothy blamed the Paris restaurant; and I think she was probably right, for it was from typhoid contracted in Paris in 1907 that Marguerite nursed him back to health before their marriage.

Dorothy could not nurse him back to health. Weeks passed; and it was not until the 26th of March that I received a telegram from her, to the effect that Bennett's condition was much worse. She urged me to come to Chiltern Court at once. I had meanwhile been asked by FitzHugh, who had the journalist's prevision, to write an appreciation of Bennett for *The Evening News*, in case he died; and this I had reluctantly done, with the hope that it would not be used. Hurrying up to London, I found the stretch of Marylebone Road outside Baker Street station spread with straw to deaden the sound of heavy traffic, and as I had not seen this old-fashioned palliative for years, the sight filled me with dread. I think that from that moment I knew there was no hope of Bennett's recovery. Going directly to the flat, I heard that he was delirious. The atmosphere of the flat was heavy with distress.

I learned afterwards that both Beaverbrook and Aldous Huxley were there. I was thrust into a larger room where members of the Bennett family, who had also been called, were assembled—his brother Frank, a white-bearded man, quite speechless, his sister Tertia and her husband William

Kennerley, whom I knew, and others I now do not clearly remember. All were very serious, for they were sure that Arnold would never again be their protector.

We talked in whispers, Tertia speaking to me with unreserved candour as Bennett's friend, and betraying the depth of her feeling, not only about Bennett, but about Dorothy and the little daughter who was being kept apart from everybody else. I had not realized before how strongly the Bennett family thought on these subjects; but almost the first words Tertia used were significant. They were 'It makes one feel so hypocritical!'—meaning that whatever sympathy she had expressed to Dorothy was insincere. She had asked what Dorothy would do if Bennett died, and Dorothy had answered 'I shall simply go on to somebody else.' This I interpreted, not, as Tertia had done, 'as a sexual partner', but 'as a backer for my ambition to become a successful producer of plays'. But there was something else which went deeper.

It was this. On the previous night, when all had gone to bed, Tertia, being still wakeful, heard unidentifiable sounds. She left her room, fearing that Bennett had reached the end, to find Dorothy and Richard together in the corridor, Richard, in pyjamas, having been summoned by Dorothy as he slept. Dorothy had impulsively seized Richard by his shoulders in order to emphasize what she was saying; and when she saw Tertia, who was dumb with amazement, she released him, exclaiming 'What an incestuous scene!' The episode was over; but memory of it, and her instinctive reaction to the coarseness, made Tertia tremble with detestation.

Now it is quite clear to me that Dorothy was not planning Richard's seduction. She thought of him as a boy, and she several times in later years reproved him for what she considered bad habits. She had merely had an afterthought; and as it had been her custom to invade Bennett's bedroom when such afterthoughts became all-important, she had followed practice. That was all, I think. It was the exclamation which disgusted Tertia. Just as Bennett was a good man, so his sister was a good woman. Suspicion of 'incest' would not have entered her mind.

At last I was taken alone into Bennett's bedroom, where he lay, flushed and restless. As I had been warned that he was delirious, I did not expect to be recognized; but something happened which I afterwards felt must have shown that he was aware of me as myself. That is, he gripped my hand in both his own, repeating, with almost frantic determination 'I will not *do* it! I will not *do* it!' He then lay still, exhausted, and did not speak again while I was there. This painful agitation in one whom I had never seen otherwise than calm was ghastly. I shall explain in a moment what I believe it meant.

I did not see Virginia that day. She was then five years old, and Bennett was devoted to her. Another sister of his, interviewed by a journalist, expressed the view that when Dorothy said he was a 'born' father she was not telling the truth. I think hostility to Dorothy misled her. As it happened, I had seen the two together on a number of occasions, and the understanding between them was amusingly notable. Virginia sat on his knee, and sometimes jogged his elbow, as he wrote; and Bennett insisted that her supposed naughtiness was natural and a sign of strong character. In looks she was, and still is, as fair as her mother; but in character she was always a true Bennett.

This visit took place on the morning of Thursday, March 26th, 1931. I called again at Chiltern Court, and had tea with Dorothy and Virginia; but did not see Bennett, who was in a coma. He died at nine o'clock that night.

15

The following morning, Saturday, March 28th, I read at breakfast the obituary notice in *The Times*, and two hours later received an urgent telegram from Dorothy, asking me to go again to Chiltern Court. I set off as soon as possible, and for some reason had to walk from Waterloo across Hungerford Bridge. I think it was in order to leave a note for my wife, who had left home before the telegram arrived, to meet a friend in town. From the Bridge I could see a newspaper seller outside the Charing Cross tube station on the Embankment below, holding an *Evening News* poster which read 'ARNOLD BENNETT BY FRANK SWINNERTON'. This gave me a most painful shock, as it suggested that I was exploiting the death of a friend. Of course I had not done so. I had been requested, as a professional journalist, to do a journalist's job. Nevertheless, pain at the loss of that friend was confused by other sensations.

I had intended to print the tribute as an Appendix to the present book; but I feel it may more appropriately come here, where it will explain what follows. This is what I had written.

Arnold Bennett was the best, the kindest, the most generous, and the greatest man with whom I had ever come into close contact. He had great sagacity, great simplicity, a good deal of most lovable vanity; and he was astoundingly modest. The better one knew him the more one loved him, and the more impressive his quality as a man became.

All his friends will agree with me as to his character, even if they deny greatness to his literary work. And all will agree that to a powerful personality, in which resoluteness, integrity, and a love of plain speaking had their obvious place, he united a charm at once mischievous and benign which many of his readers must have missed.

Strangers often formed very different opinions from these. They were sometimes a little frightened by his reputation. They misconstrued his abruptness of manner. They found him assertive and inflexible. And they believed the legend that he was a man who had mapped out his life with the sole object of amassing money. Many of them resented his success. But I do not know anybody who was indifferent to him.

Let me try to give some notion of what Arnold Bennett looked like. He was stoutly built and about five feet ten inches in height. He held himself very erect and his shoulders very rigid, so that his body had no natural swing as he walked, but rather swayed stiffly from side to side. He always walked slowly and with great seriousness.

His brow was square and rose straight from eyes that looked tired, because of rather heavy eyelids, to the small flourish of hair which latterly replaced the famous coif made fun of by caricaturists. His cheeks were clear and showed a faint colour. His mouth was irregular and his upper teeth also irregular.

The eyes, once the first impression of tiredness had passed, were a warm brown, and smiled. Bennett was a master of the wink. When some effusive stranger buttonholed him to express admiration, Bennett was at all times courteous; but, if he caught a friendly eye beyond his enthusiast, one of those heavy lids would irresistibly quiver.

In repose his expression, I should have said, represented calm melancholy. But his smile was very sweet, and the aura of kindness which surrounded him was such that he was extremely popular with children. Odd as it may seem to some, he could converse with children very effectively. But he was a shy and sensitive man, who normally talked little.

When I first knew him, he once referred to Mr H. G. Wells's unlimited brilliance as a conversationalist by saying briefly: 'He talks, you know. I can't do that.' And in those days he could not, or did not, talk. When pressed for an opinion by guests at his own table, he would often jerk his head in my direction, and say: '*He'll* tell you.'

One day I said to him: 'I talk too much.' He said: 'Yes; but from politeness.' It was politeness that caused Bennett to talk more freely in later years. He did not really enjoy talking. But he talked to entertain his guests, to 'make things go,' and he did this very well, though sometimes with exaggeration of his own mannerisms.

And I am here reminded to mention a fact which explains much about Bennett which has puzzled and irritated his less sympathetic readers. I have said that he was exceptionally shy and sensitive. He stammered. It was not a slight stammer; but when he was at all agitated the stammer became a complete inhibition of speech.

So strong was his will that he always persisted in fighting the stammer until he could pronounce the word he had in mind; but these struggles often caused disconcerting delays and silences, and their possibility was ever present in his mind. Hence his abruptness, which communicated itself to his writing, and gave that writing an air of dogmatism.

He would say, if his opinion were challenged: 'I can't argue.' It was often thought that he disdained argument. This was not the case. He argued with his intimates; but with his intimates he rarely stammered, unless he had something painful to tell them.

His voice was rather harsh, and gave the impression of being high-pitched. His manner was, to friends, genial. Very often, one would catch sight of him from a little distance, seated, very carefully smoking a cigarette. Probably making a note in a tiny notebook which he always carried. His expression would be grave.

But as one approached he would look up. 'Hello, boss,' he would say, saluting with a finger to his forelock. Or, if one had a surname which he liked to pronounce, but which offered difficulties to his tongue, he would *say* the first letters with mock ceremoniousness—as 'Well, Mister S-W-I-innerton.' Comparatively few people, except in company, called him 'Arnold.' To innumerable friends, old and young, he was 'A.B.' It was as if they used a diminutive.

And his friends really were innumerable. They were absolutely sure of his interest and his integrity. They went to him with all sorts of petitions, troubles, confessions. He listened to them at length; then he gave his advice. He corresponded with them—hundreds of them. He was always ready to help them, and did so, with money, encouragement, and sympathy.

Sometimes he would refer to one of them as 'he'. 'That chap,' he would say. A pause. A jerk of the head. Then: 'He has to be *helped*.' And he *was* helped. Once, when I had received an appeal, and had shown him the letter, he said (though he did not know the applicant): 'What are you going to send! I should like to do the same!' And out popped one of the odd cheques which he always carried for emergencies.

He came, as is well known, from Staffordshire; and I think his first interest in myself (otherwise a literary interest) arose from the fact that mine is a Staffordshire name. He was born a Methodist. And in spite of the fact that intellectually he was an agnostic he remained essentially a Methodist (and a Midlander) all his life.

The sneers of some people (who had not learned courtesy in the course of an otherwise elaborate curriculum) at his 'provincialism' had no truth so far as his intellect and his imagination were concerned. He was provincial in the sense that the Provinces, the backbone of England, are provincial. He also retained certain provincialisms of speech and pronunciation (I only mean in such words as 'bath' or 'ask', in which he used the light 'a', and such phrases as his favourite 'We shall look a bit soft').

He was easily impressed by magnificence or by a display of knowledge. I think he could at times be caught by the second-rate. But only for a time, for his judgment was in constant repair, and his scrutiny was very unsentimental. Otherwise, when he was thought 'provincial', he was often just humorous. As for example when he moved into a house where the panels of all the doors had been decorated by a former tenant with mirrors. At my first visit to this house I said, 'Oh, Lord! I couldn't stand all this looking-glass!' He replied, blandly, 'I was born for it!'

He dressed with great care. His shirts were always superfine. Once, when he dined in company with a very great personage, the personage broke a long silence by saying: 'Mr Bennett; do you mind if I ask you something?' Bennett agreed to be asked something. 'Do you mind telling me where you get your shirts?'

It was a great moment. I can imagine the wave of Bennett's hand—for he used, deliberately, a good deal of not always graceful gesture—as he responded. That was what I meant in referring to his lovable vanity. He could be, and was, teased endlessly as to his clothes; but he did give them a great deal of thought. As a consequence he was always described by *The Tailor and Cutter* as 'the best-dressed author in London.'

What interested him most of all, however, was not clothes. Nor was it talk. He had a really passionate interest in human nature; and a really passionate love of the fine arts. You had only to look at his beautiful and sensitive hands (of which I never knew him to be conscious) to realize a delicacy for which his manner might not have prepared you; only to be in his company during the performance of music or before pictures, to realize that power he had of yielding himself completely to beauty.

He was not a systematic critic, but was purely intuitive. As a result, some of the opinions he expressed on particular artists or particular works were erratic. The elegant often shivered at his judgments. On the whole, however, these judgments (unless they were roundly stated, when it was wise to suspect them) wore well, and will wear well.

He was a little bitten with the desire to be up to date. Not in private. Some of his friends used to tease him about his pronouncements. He was always ready for such gibes; and equal to them. And at the end of a bout of opposed statements either the opinions did not seem so eccentric, or Bennett would remark: 'Well, there may be something in what you say.' Immediately afterwards, recovering himself, he would add: 'But not much.' He would never yield to argument; but he would listen to it 'with due respect.'

Not always, though. Several years ago, the date of Marie Lloyd's birth became a subject of dispute between us. I said she was born in 1870. Bennett said I was wrong; that she must have been born much earlier. I insisted. He said: 'We'll soon settle it. I've got all the reference books in my study.' He disappeared. Ten minutes later, he returned. 'Extraordinary!' said he. 'I've looked in a dozen books. And they're ALL wrong!'

But he was laughing as he spoke. His downrightness—when not due to his stammer—was largely an innocent pose. He was also, as I have said (the remark may have caused some rubbing of eyes), an excessively modest man. He never spoke of his own books, though often of the number of words he had written that day. He accepted printed criticism (though it was sometimes violent) better than any other author I have ever known. His response to private praise, when he took it seriously, was one of surprise and pleasure.

Indeed, as a proof of his modesty, I recall that once, when somebody, not myself, had repeated quite reasonable praise of his work, he meditatively said: 'Well, it's odd, but I can't see it!' This was the truth. In public he always pretended to be delighted with his own performance.

His greatest vanity was that he was a man-of-the-world. He was never a man-of-the-world. He had not the pulpy sentimentality veneered with cynicism that is characteristic of that species. He was, on the contrary, once he went outside his own shrewd, practical genius, simple almost to *naïveté*.

He had the loving heart of a good man, plus the sensitiveness of the artist, the efficient mind of the practical thinker, the timidity of the stammerer, the determination of the midlander, the rigour of the moralist, and the generosity of greatness. I think he was a great writer, but he was a greater man.

As for his personality, it is not without significance that he came from the same county as Doctor Johnson. It was his habit to say that 'nine out of every ten people improve on acquaintance,' and the more one knew Arnold Bennett the more one marvelled at the sympathy, the patience, the large tolerance, and the essential sweetness and simplicity which were the sources of his strength and of the affection of his friends.

March 28, 1931

16

When I reached Chiltern Court on that Saturday morning I found Dorothy in considerable distress, not so much on account of Bennett's death, for which she had been prepared, but because she felt herself to have been deserted by his friends and his family. In particular, she complained that Wells, living only two or three floors above her in the same building, had not once visited her during Bennett's illness, and even this morning had not made any attempt to communicate with her. She felt that in view of a friendship which had begun in 1897 and continued unbroken for more than thirty years Wells should have been the first to come to her help.

She did not weep. She was quite composed. Her chief thought, apart from resentment at neglect, seemed to be that without Bennett's income she would be in a financial difficulty; but she had hopes that the doctor would not present a bill and that Beaverbrook, as a rich man, would provide for her.

Before I left, she suggested that she and I should go into the room where Bennett lay; and as we entered it she spoke some reproachful words, addressing him as 'Little,' the name with which his more intimate letters were signed. He was lying, much shrunken, with absolutely white cheeks and the weary eyes closed. He was entirely at peace; and this glimpse of death was very affecting. As we gazed, however, Dorothy caught sight of the translucent brandy-coloured ring which he always wore on the little finger of his left hand. To my horror, she moved quickly across the room, wrenched the ring from his finger, and said 'I'm sure he'd wish me to have this.'

There was no suggestion that the ring was to be a treasured keepsake. She was appropriating something she fancied.

There remained the question of Wells. The two men were almost exact contemporaries, Wells having been born on September 21st, 1866 and Bennett on May 27th, 1867. Wells was the son of an unsuccessful little shopkeeper, Bennett the son of an unsuccessful solicitor turned pawnbroker. They had much in common, the prime similarity between them being amusement at the foibles of other men. It was a Victorian trait, free from the spiteful satire of a later generation; and Wells once told me, as a marvel, that Bennett and G. K. Chesterton were the only contemporary writers with whom he had not, at some time or other, quarrelled.

Some pepperiness in his disposition made him, for all his merriment, liable to take offence; and when he did this, as for example with Henry James, he retorted upon those whose disagreement he resented in sharp letters and even, as in *Boon*, where he compared James's' art to that of a hippopotamus picking up a pea, in lampoons. But, he said, he had never had a cross word with the two he named. He could not account for it except as the result of mutual affection.

A long time afterwards, when we were speaking of Wells, I mentioned to Bennett what Wells had said. Bennett answered, with no stammer, 'He tried to, with me. I wouldn't let him.'

The two men were very good fun when together, Wells with his darting quickness but affectionate mercy towards those he liked, Bennett with unruffled calm. I remember being in their company when Bennett announced a decision. Said he 'Ferrero's *History of Rome* is a *great* book.' Wells said 'No, Arnold, *not* a great book. A *brilliant* book.' I said 'H.G.'s afraid of brilliance', and Bennett retorted 'It will be his ruin yet.'

Because this was my abiding impression of their delightful association, I thought Dorothy's plaint was justified. I told her so. She begged me to go upstairs and see Wells, and to ask if he would come down and visit her. We had some further conversation, which I have forgotten (I think she said Beaverbrook was trying hard to persuade the Dean of Westminster that Bennett's burial in the Abbey would be proper); and I then left her.

I found Wells sitting at his desk with *The Evening News* spread before him. There were tears on his cheeks. He said

'I've been reading what you wrote about Arnold, Swinny. It's moved me very much.' I then told him of my last meeting with Bennett, and gave him Dorothy's message. He almost screamed 'No! I *won't*! She's a bitch; and she killed Arnold!'

There was no more to be said.

17

I wish now to mention two or three details which I only *believe* to be true. They occurred to me after conversation with Winifred Nerney, who was well informed of all that took place in the Bennett household. I should emphasize the fact that she was not a malicious woman. She was extremely straightforward in both writing and speaking, a small (but in no sense tiny) woman of resolution and great good sense, who knew that Bennett had complete confidence in me and who felt similar confidence.

She told me what she would not have told anybody else; and before she died she sent me, as Bennett's friend, considerable quantities of letters and other papers which she might have destroyed but which she rightly thought I should value. I have read and re-read many of these letters and papers, some of which I have quoted or shall quote. They include letters from Bennett to herself, letters from herself to Bennett which he has annotated, letters to and from Tertia Kennerley, and many more, all of the highest interest. In the past months they have reminded me vividly of what happened long ago.

The reader will remember that, on his return from France at the beginning of 1931 Bennett wished to see me alone; and that on the day he suggested I was engaged to lunch with George Doran, our American publisher. Also that on the day alternatively fixed he was too ill, supposedly with influenza, to keep our appointment. Therefore we did not meet until the day before his death, when he gripped my hand convulsively as he exclaimed 'I will not *do* it!'

At that time I was unaware of two things which Winifred Nerney reported later. The first was Bennett's determination to bring Dorothy back from France a changed woman; the second that this resolve followed a demand from Dorothy for an allowance equal to Marguerite's as the price of a separation —namely, a guaranteed two thousand pounds a year.

It was alleged by Dorothy that Bennett's last delirious words to herself were 'The bill! The bill!' and this cry was uncharitably assumed by one anonymous commentator to mean that in his very last hours Bennett, the money-worshipper, was thinking of cash. The charge seemed to Winifred Nerney so monstrous that she ascertained the name of this commentator and wrote to him correcting the misinterpretation. I do not know whether her protest had any effect: the charge was never withdrawn, and Bennett's memory was sullied once again in the eyes of that particular commentator's readers. Winifred Nerney knew the truth. As for myself, I can only say what twenty years of close acquaintance with Bennett leads me to infer from those last words.

I think Bennett had reached the point of absolute resistance to a personality which, however energetic, was not, as his was, fundamentally reasonable; and that in spite of his love for Virginia, who was being used by her mother as a pawn, he knew that he and Dorothy must part. I think that just as he had come to me when the break with Marguerite occurred so he wanted to discuss with the same person (whom he always described to others as 'sagacious') this second break. It was a misfortune that the proposed meeting did not take place.

I am not a doctor, versed in the behaviour of men about to die. I only assume that in delirium essential preoccupations struggle for release; and that while the delirious person may not positively recognize an individual some chord is touched by the contact or by a familiar voice which produces startling disclosures. To myself, as a former confidant, he was saying that he would not submit to Dorothy's demand; to Dorothy, although she did not understand it, he was indicating that she would get no more of him—not merely in money, but in love.

This, as I have said, is what I believe. I am not a fanciful man, and not a sensationalist. I cannot now submit my opinion to either of the two women, Winifred Nerney and Pauline Smith, who could have offered their judgment on what I have just written. Both are dead. But Winifred, close to Bennett during those last months and last scenes, told me many facts;

while Pauline, at a distance, might have received from Bennett, by letter, some notification of what was going on. He did, unquestionably, and for years, keep her informed of his private affairs. The letters he wrote her were all, by mutual agreement, destroyed as soon as they had been read.

Pauline, as far as I remember, kept her opinions of Marguerite and Dorothy in her sweet and mysterious mind—except for one disclosure which I shall now reveal. She was devoted to Bennett, as her charming little book *A.B.: a Minor Marginal Note* reveals; and in that book she explains how their acquaintance began in Switzerland, where she and her mother and sister chanced to be staying at the same small hotel in the hills above Vevey as Bennett and Marguerite.

'At dinner on the night of their arrival the elegance of his wife, and the rather jaunty swagger with which, all his life, he sought to hide his own secret diffidence, caused much comment among his fellow-guests.' Some conversation ensued between Bennett and Pauline's mother, arising from Mrs Smith's discovery that Bennett must be the 'Jacob Tonson' who was carrying on, in *The New Age*, an argument with 'Claudius Clear' (Dr Robertson Nicoll) in *The British Weekly*. In the course of this conversation he learned that Pauline 'wrote a little.' He thereupon insisted upon seeing what she had written, and he was shown a number of short stories and the first chapters of a novel. The chapters he damned; but the short stories, which came out in after years as *Platkops Children*, he praised. He demanded that the young woman should go on writing. Pauline, who was very shy, had no realization of her own talent; but the effect of his encouragement (she said the way in which he damned the early chapters of her novel gave her 'an overwhelming sense of relief and release') was so great that she struggled to earn more of it.

Nor did Bennett content himself with private advice. In time he arranged, through Pinker, the literary agent, for the publication by Jonathan Cape of *The Little Karoo*, for which he wrote a preface; and on the strength of this book Pauline is seen in South Africa as a writer who has profoundly expressed the spirit of poor people in that land. Her letters to me are preserved at Wittwatersrand University, where many a student, I hope, will endeavour to decipher them. It will be no easy task.

In Switzerland, always what is called a perfectionist, she paused, and hesitated, and re-wrote so much that in spite of persistent inquiries and exhortations she made little visible progress with her exquisite work. Bennett, on the contrary, then at the height of self-confidence as a result of the success of *The Old Wive's Tale*, dashed off *The Card* by means of steady work and his ability to write in any circumstances whatever.

It was a sign of his regard for Pauline that he presented her with the original manuscript of this book, with the inscription:

> 'THE CARD, called in America "Denry the Audacious", written by Arnold Bennett in January and February, 1909, at Mont Pelerin in the immediate proximity of Pauline and other friends of Claudius Clear. This manuscript, saved from the waste-paper basket by a pious wife, is given to the said Pauline by the said wife as a token that some novels do get finished somehow.'
>
> M.M.B. A.B.

The manuscript naturally became one of Pauline's treasures, for Bennett's manuscripts were always beautiful, and the character of Edward Henry Machin makes it one of the most amusing books he ever wrote. She kept it with care. After Bennett's death, however, she expressed to me the fear that in spite of the inscription Dorothy might run off with it. The fear showed her previously hidden judgment, as well as her inexperience and incapacity for combat; and she said 'I meant to leave it to you in my will; but I shall feel safer if I give it to you now.' My reply was 'Why not do as I should do if you left it to me in your will—give it to the Manuscripts Department at the British Museum?' Pauline regarded this as inspiration, and was overjoyed; and I at once made the arrangement on her behalf. She received such an enthusiastic letter of thanks from the Museum authorities that she was tempted, she said, to compose a return letter of thanks for their jubilance. Everybody had been made happy; and the manuscript of *The Card* had been saved from one whose acquisitiveness was thus proclaimed and defeated.

One curious fact remains. When Bennett's manuscripts and correspondence were sold at Sotherby's in 1936 all the letters from Pauline to Bennett were bought in for thirty shillings by Dorothy.

18

I have already said that Alistair ('Duff') Tayler in the first instance, as Executor, paid the Death Duties on Bennett's estate out of his own pocket. He was forced, also, owing to Dorothy's habit of returning to the Chiltern Court flat to collect other small items of her choice, to change the lock on the front door, and he was a greatly worried man. He even considered taking legal action against both Marguerite and Dorothy for the recovery of his outlay. The estate was valued at thirty thousand pounds; but this consisted chiefly of an arbitrary valuation of Bennett's copyrights. The amount of cash available was relatively small.

Dorothy had acquired a house which she was sub-letting to other tenants. She was alarmed, however, to discover that she had contravened a clause in her lease by this sub-letting; and having no available income other than the interest from the Trust she was very nearly desperate. Her application for help from, among others, Beaverbrook, Shaw, and Wells, was unsuccessful. Her suggestion that I should ask members of the Reform Club circle to subscribe fifteen hundred pounds on her behalf produced no result. In those circumstances, since she could not touch the Trust capital, she was full of plans to re-invest this capital in stocks bearing higher rates of interest; and I received many letters from her naming shares which I was advised were unsound.

My resistance to these plans was fortunately buttressed by the fact that we were forbidden by the terms of the Trust to invest in any but gilt-edged securities. Otherwise I might have become liable to pay inevitable losses, a possibility that filled me with dread. My letters, no doubt, were pacific; but during all these discussions Dorothy behaved with great restraint, never losing her temper (although she claimed to be a financial wizard); and going so far as to propose that, in the event of her death, my wife and I should act as guardians for Virginia. We gladly agreed to do this; and I only heard later that we should have been bound by all sorts of stupilations and conditions as they suggested themselves to a fertile imagination. In the end the investments were not changed, and the Trust remained intact.

Her next plan was to return to the United States, where she hoped to produce the French play and two of Bennett's own plays. She was given much publicity in America, and obtained a brief engagement as an actress. Thus encouraged, she resolved to stay in the New World; but Virginia had to be considered. She had been left in charge of her nurse, Mrs Hodges, who was devoted to the little girl, and would gladly have kept on looking after her. Unfortunately Dorothy was sure that no nurse could take a mother's place, and for some reason which I never understood she insisted that Virginia should be dispatched to her in charge of a stewardess on the *Aquitania*.

The scheme immediately aroused opposition. Mrs Hodges protested; and was over-ruled. Others did the same, with a similar result. Tertia, in particular, was outraged. She wrote to Winifred Nerney on April 18th, 1933:

> 'I went to see Virginia on her birthday, and found her well and happy and delightful. Also Mrs Hodges, just as you said. We had a good old talk. It amused me ironically that after a good while she asked me (excusing herself for doing so) if I was a real relation or an Aunt *a la* you or Pauline. Well, Miss Nerney, after all (unless by now there is another change) the child is to sail for America on the 29th. Mrs Hodges is fed up about it—says she has done her best and can't push it further lest Dorothy thinks she keeps her for the sake of the money. The child is to go in care of a stewardess. Virginia had her hand in mine when Mrs Hodges spoke about it first, and her instinctive grip and dead silence convinced me that she shrinks from going. Mrs Hodges told me that one time Virginia went to her and said "I can come and live with you any time I want, can't I?" Can't anything be done? I've thought and thought. My advice to

Mrs Hodges is to miss the boat. I know if I had her Dorothy might cable until she was blue and I should take no notice. I have thought of Mr Swinnerton and Mr Tayler, and finally of Lord Beaverbrook. It is unthinkable that Virginia should be sent off like that, and she so happily installed where she is. Mrs Hodges was most thankful to meet a sane *real* relation, and has my London address and my Bognor one. I think of going down again with Mrs Beardmore, who said she wanted very much to see Virginia. She doesn't yet know of the American idea. Do for Heaven's sake think what can be done. You are the only person who can write to Dorothy saying she is not sailing. Let Dorothy fetch her if she must have her. Hotel life, rushing around America, in addition to the journey, new nurses, scenes, scenes, and scenes. My love to your mother. Yours sincerely,

Tertia Kennerley.

Winifred replied at length to this letter on the following day, April 19th, 1933.

'Thank you so much for your letter. I am so glad you got down to see Virginia, and she must have been delighted. Isn't she a dear kid.

I had a letter from D.C.B. saying that Virginia was to sail on the *Aquitania* on the 29th, and intimating to me that she knew better than I did what was good for V. and what the conditions were like for children in New York. Also, that as rehearsals for the play will be over (it was produced on the 17th) she is taking Virginia to stay at one of the country houses to which they are invited. So that's that, and I do not see what more can be done, as she is the one person with the right to say whether V. shall go or not. Mr Swinnerton has already cabled about it, and I do not think would want to do so again, and it would be useless for Lord Beaverbrook or any other of Mr Bennett's friends to interfere, even if they would do so, as they have never shown the slightest interest in the child or her welfare, and she might be starving for all they know. They make the excuse that it is because of the mother, ignoring the fact that she is also Mr Bennett's daughter and he frequently helped people, and on that score one might reasonably expect some interest and kindness from them. I may cable again, but feel it will probably do more harm than good.'

There is much more in the letter, which Winifred herself described as 'truculent' and an 'outburst'; but I shall leave it unquoted because it is critical of named persons who need not be pilloried. Virginia did indeed sail on the *Aquitania*, in charge of a stewardess, and spent what she has described to me as a most unnatural childhood with her mother, exactly as Tertia had imagined it would be.

19

The stay in America did not last long. Theatrical ventures proved unrewarding; and another situation arose which compelled a return to England. Marguerite, finding her own comfortable living in jeopardy, and hot with resentment against an upstart, proceeded to claim the manuscripts, journals, and copyrights which Bennett, with great ceremony, had handed over to Dorothy.

He described the transaction in his *Journal* for 1928:

> 'Tuesday, December 18th. Today . . . I formally gave to Dorothy 47 volumes of my mss. (34 of *Journal*, 2 *Old Wives' Tale*, 1 *Riceyman Steps*, 1 *Elsie*, and 9 *Clayhanger Family*) in the presence of Miss Nerney, Fred Harvey [his butler], Swinnerton, and Geoffrey Russell.'

There is no doubt at all that he made this presentation before witnesses on the advice of Geoffrey Russell, his solicitor and an easily ruffled member of the Reform Club circle; and that it was intended to forestall any claim that Marguerite might make to the property and rights. Marguerite protested that, as his legitimate wife, she was entitled, notwithstanding the gift, to enjoy possession of everything her husband left. She included in her claim the sum invested on behalf of Virginia, so that I, too, was involved. She at first expressed, quite moderately, willingness to accept a solatium of two hundred pounds; but when difficulty arose increased her demand to a thousand pounds. When this was refused, she instituted legal proceedings against Dorothy and myself as Trustees for Virginia's heritage.

I must explain that she refused to believe that Virginia was Bennett's child, a fact which gave me a possible explanation of her constant fretfulness and moody silences during their married life. That is, I wondered whether, although Bennett was sexually normal, he might not have been, in her case, what George Gissing called 'sexually prefulgent'. I have no evidence at all for this; it is pure surmise, and natural jealousy of another woman may have been the sole basis for her conduct.

Dorothy, for her part, feeling deserted by all Bennett's friends but myself, sought advice on the question by engaging in spiritualist seances. She asserted that in these Bennett had strongly urged her to resist Marguerite's demands. So the case came to Court.

We shared one solicitor, although Dorothy urged me to employ another, more energetic man; and our advocate addressed me in almost fulsome terms. He said 'You're my witness! I can't put *her* in the box!' He evidently did not trust Dorothy; and I must have given my evidence in good order; for while I was still under cross-examination the opposing Counsel interrupted to say that his client wished to withdraw all claims against me. The Judge spoke learned words. They were 'I'm glad of that, Sir William. You wouldn't have got it, you know.' So I was dismissed from the case.

Dorothy and I went to the back of the Court, where she clung to me, speaking in a whisper, and evidently wishing to comment upon what had happened. I could not hear her, for I was listening to what a hair-splitting Junior Counsel was asserting. He had in his hand the *Journal* in which Bennett had written 'Today . . . I formally gave to Dorothy 47 volumes of my mss;' and he insisted that the word 'formally' meant no more than 'as a matter of form.' I exclaimed 'He mustn't be allowed to get away with that'—meaning that Bennett had used the word 'formally' in the sense of 'with due ceremony.' Dorothy, who had not listened, continued to cling and whisper. It was a long way from where we stood to the front of the Court. Our barrister made no protest. The Judge accepted the argument. Dorothy lost the case.

The question of an Appeal was considered. I was against it; but Dorothy persisted. She was quite right to do so; and the Judge's decision was reversed. Marguerite was declared the loser. Dorothy therefore retained the manuscripts, as Bennett had intended that she should do. She made no reproach to me at all for my opposition to the Appeal. We remained on good terms as before. And if it had been possible for him to do so Bennett would have turned in his grave at the mess resulting from what he had done with his love of organization and precise statement.

20

I think it a pity that, as a rule, Bennett's biographers never met the man whose life and character they seek to re-create. They approach him through a mist of poisonous vapour spread by snobs who sought to discredit a thoroughly 'decent' man. Bennett, unlike his detractors, had no streak of cruelty in his disposition. Of some men he would occasionally remark, with a shaken head, 'No good'; but he never attacked with the object of causing pain or injuring reputation.

His criticism of friends was all spoken or written to themselves; not slipped in behind their backs or by innuendo. A. G. Gardiner, whom we both liked very much, once remarked 'I know you say I'm conceited, Arnold'; and after the familiar drawled 'We . . ell' came the quick 'of course you *are.*' It was said with such obvious kindness that everybody, including Gardiner, laughed heartily. Gardiner, retorting in the same spirit, wrote a short study in which he maintained that there were two Bennetts, Arnold the sophisticate and Enoch the lovable lad from the Potteries. He naturally preferred Enoch, but failed to see that Arnold, far from being sophisticated (however he deceived himself), was everybody's father, anxious that no man should ever commit a *cliché*, whether in composition or in thought.

This fatherliness expressed itself in disapproving statements, as when introducing me to others, he once said 'He is hard. He is crewel. Aand . . . he is idle.' But even the malicious busybodies who like to repeat to their colleagues the unkind things said about them by others could bring me no tales of adverse comment by him. This was not a question of attachment, for he never failed in candour if he thought I had acted or written amiss: it was the man himself, humorously downright to one's face, generous elsewhere.

I remember another novelist, of lesser note but given to writing about his contemporaries, boasting that he spoke no ill of any man. He added, however, 'unless they've slated me, or one of my friends.' He was familiar with all literary cliques and cabals, and meant no harm; but he created and perpetuated feuds, always simmering among a touchy breed, and could not be relied on for discretion if tempted to belittle other men. There was nothing of this sort about Bennett. He was above all spitefulness. How sad that he should so often have aroused the spitefulness of lesser men!

It is true that he continued throughout life to use provincial words and pronunciations. He would say, if too early for an appointment, 'We shall look a bit soft,' or 'I said I would go to bed at ten o'clock; aand I *did* do.' Whereas I and others put an 'h' sound into the words 'dance' or 'bath', he used the flat 'a' for all such words. Otherwise he spoke without affectation, and would not have dreamed of pronouncing 'frost' as 'frawst' or 'gone' as 'gorn', as Cockneys and bogus gentry do.

He had foibles. Having lived for some years in France with a French wife, he often used a French word in his letters or in speech when an English word would have served—for example, '*déséquilibré*' instead of 'unbalanced', or '*coquille*' instead of 'misprint'. There was no affectation in this; it was a habit arising from familiarity with two languages. All the same it amused his friends.

Another foible was his interest in clothes. I have quoted a letter to Winifred Nerney giving directions about a new dress for Rose, the parlourmaid who must look 'smart'. In that letter he says he has seen a number of smart dresses in the shops, and he must have taken an interest in such things, as he did in everything (were not several of his books of collected trifles called *Things that have interested me*?); and male 'attire', as he liked to call it, was a subject of much concern. This was so great that, when being fitted with a new suit, he transferred from the pockets of older garments all protrusive belongings, so that the new clothes should take account of them. In the end his tailors told him he was more trouble than he was worth, a verdict which, although mystified by it, he accepted with naïve patience.

One day, walking down Oxford Street, he saw in the window of a shop an extraordinary show of straw hats, of the kind formerly known as 'boaters'. A notice accompanying this display announced that each of these hats could be bought for four shillings and elevenpence, which, as the hats were 'smart', was very cheap indeed. Conquering his diffidence, he went into the shop. His salesman, expert at the job, and sighting a man of means, produced hats selling at a guinea or more. Here was a dilemma! If he had yielded to weakness, he would have accepted one of these more expensive hats; but, nerving himself to bravery, he blurted out 'I want one of those four and elevenpenny hats'. The courage shown was rewarded. He bore away the hat in triumph, and it became his *panache*, almost a Victoria Cross 'for valour'.

Soon afterwards, when H. W. Massingham and I were spending the weekend at Dover, on board the *Marie Marguerite*, and the weather was threatening, we all arranged to walk about the town. Bennett was protected by a magnificent oilskin outer garment. Just as we started he hesitated, saying 'Now, shall I wear my new four and elevenpenny straw hat?' I rudely answered 'You can't possibly wear a straw hat with that rig!' He was at once cowed. 'Can't I, Guv? I just thought it might be a little more . . . *smart*!' He submissively put on his sou'wester.

When I was fourteen years old I was office boy in the London branch of some Scottish periodical publishers; and every week I delivered copies of the firm's periodicals, *The Scottish Cyclist* and *St. Andrew*, to advertising agents and others in the City and West End. I enjoyed my journeys, which enabled me to glance into shop-windows; and among the most interesting windows were those in a sort of bay between Essex Street and Arundel Street, Strand, of *The Graphic* and *The Illustrated London News*, where wash drawings and photographs used in the papers were exhibited. One day I noticed something unfamiliar. It was the copy of a paper I had never seen, boastfully called, because of its price, *The Golden Penny*. On the cover of this paper were the words 'Great Serial Story by a New Author'. There followed in large letters, the title *The Grand Babylon Hotel*, and the author's name, which was Arnold Bennett.

I did not buy *The Golden Penny*. My wages were only six shillings a week. But for some reason the title and the author's name stayed in memory. I found it again in 1907 when I began to work for the firm which had published both *The Grand Babylon Hotel* and *Anna of the Five Towns* in the same year, 1901. The two books represented two sides of Bennett's production; and purists have suggested that the former showed him to be a literary prostitute, writing for money, and the latter the beginning of his study of the Five Towns.

The truth about *The Grand Babylon Hotel* is quite otherwise. When he was Editor of *Woman*, one of Bennett's tasks was to buy serial stories for his paper. These serials were usually mediocre; and one day he said as much to the representative of the Syndicate providing them. He remarked 'I could do better myself'. The representative answered 'Why don't you?' Thus challenged, Bennett wrote a serial. Philip Gibbs, acting for the Syndicate, as he told me many years later, laughing with his complete freedom from malice, was empowered to offer a hundred pounds or more for *The Grand Babylon Hotel.* He interviewed the author and offered seventy-five pounds for all rights in the book. Bennett accepted the cut price without bargaining; and Gibbs, who admired the book very much, had made a most satisfactory deal for his employers. He continued to rejoice innocently in the thought that, much as he loved Bennett, he had made a splendid bargain.

The Syndicate proceeded to sell volume rights to Andrew Chatto, who made a practice of buying copyrights, as he had done in the cases of Hall Caine, Walter Besant, and many more. Bennett received no further payments. He had responded in the first instance to a challenge; he had delivered the goods; he made no complaint; merely warned fellow-authors against a young man with nicotine-stained fingers, a description which caused Gibbs, a great cigarette smoker, to feel delighted amusement.

So much for the legend that Bennett wrote pot-boilers from a love of money. Other men can do no better. He was different. He wrote the books he called 'larks' simply because his fertile humorous inventiveness, which in non-stammering men, such as myself, is released in conversation, had no other outlet. He could not talk; so he wrote *A Great Man*, *Buried Alive*, and *The Card* at high speed, for fun, and probably received no more than advances of seventy-five pounds on account of royalties. The so-called pot-boilers, *The Ghost*, *The City of Pleasure*, and *The Gates of Wrath*, all produced in young manhood, satisfied a romanticism otherwise repressed.

As readers will remember, he was an active journalist all his life, and a man who believed in what he called 'organization'. He grew up at a time, now forgotten, when intelligent youngsters were trying to educate themselves by reading the 'classics', and being supplied by publishers with reprints of famous books at prices ranging from a penny to three-shillings-and-sixpence. Bennett, better 'organized' than the majority of half-educated young clerks, felt that they 'needed to be helped'. Having been trained in elder-brotherly care for his juniors, he was well-equipped to advise self-improvers for their own good.

Among his journalistic compositions, therefore, were articles for *T.P.'s Weekly*, a periodical launched by T. P. O'Connor for those of imperfect education who had a love of books; and these articles were collected in a series called by the publishers 'pocket philosophies'. They had such titles as *How to Live on Twenty-four Hours a Day* and *Literary Taste; and how to Form it*, and were written for small fees and with a real desire to assist the ignorant.

Intellectual aristocrats were in no need, they felt, of assistance. So they scorned Bennett's elder-brotherliness, and have done so until this day. It is unimaginative of them; but Bennett would have been the last person to utter a reproach. He was so extraordinarily modest that when he heard of John Galsworthy having presented the manuscripts of *The Forsyte Saga* to the British Museum he was outraged. He said 'It seems to me . . . to be . . . *cheek*!' When he came to London as a poor young solicitor's clerk he lodged in the same house as several other young men—Frederick Marriott, whom he called 'the worst artist in the world', Charles Young, a booksellers' assistant who became Manager of Lamley's of Kensington, and others—and he was naïvely astonished to find that his companions expected him to become an author. He did not see himself in this part, although he was proud of skill in making up a solicitor's account to any client; but he did not wish to disappoint his friends. 'I try to please everybody,' he confessed. So he wrote a few articles on subjects relating to the Law, and when these had been printed he was visited by the sudden resolve to write a novel. *A Man from the North* was the result.

It never occurred to him, at the age of thirty, when royalties on this book had paid for its typing and a new hat, that in another ten years he was to produce *The Old Wives' Tale* and become world-famous. Nor did he over-rate his gifts after that success. I was with him when he attentively read a severe verdict upon something he had written, and commented 'That . . . is awfully able!'

Finally I must report that after lunch one day at the Royal Thames Yacht Club (which he always referred to, if he wrote from there, as '80 Pic', we strolled together to Piccadilly Circus, discussing an author whom we both admired 'this side idolatry'. We were about to part when I said 'The trouble is, that when I read Tchekov I feel it's no good writing any more'. He stopped dead, stared at me, and exclaimed '*You* feel that? So do I!'

21

As old novelists used to say, in beginning their last chapters, 'The rest is soon told'. I do not propose to hurry this chapter, although I am very tired and uncertain as to whether I have fallen into the old man's sin (also his dread) of repetition. I have tried to depict Arnold Bennett as a man of character and integrity, a fundamentally innocent humorist, a superlative friend, and, to others, not myself, a difficult personality; but I have worked under considerable difficulties, with many interruptions, and the result may be unsatisfactory. If it is, I shall be sorry. One of my problems has arisen from the fact that to live again, as I have done, in a period long past and full of painful memories, has proved agitating and therefore exhausting.

Having had to struggle with Dorothy's attempts to change the stocks in which Virginia's Trust Fund were invested, I eventually relinquished my Trusteeship in favour of an Insurance Company named in the Deed. Though reluctant to accept my proposal, Dorothy consented to the change; and I never heard what happened thereafter. In 1935 she returned to the United States; and what she did there, apart from struggling with theatrical plans and making Virginia extremely unhappy, I do not know. Virginia's upbringing has been described to me as 'absolutely savage and isolated'. Having known Dorothy, and heard so much of her behaviour from Winifred Nerney, I do not doubt the truth of the description. In the midst of a wild skirmish with the theatre, she gave her attention to many branches of literature, psychology, and even the occult. Everything was superficial, energetic, and unruly. But I had no part in her life, and no personal knowledge of her activities. For the purpose of this book I do not think my ignorance really matters.

I have taken the narrative up to Bennett's death and its immediate sequels. Now I must add other information for the sake of perspective. I never saw Marguerite after the separation. She wrote to me several times from Negrepelisse, where she settled, and paid several visits to the Kennerleys, in Sussex; but she had not met my wife, and there was no occasion for a meeting. I renewed acquaintance with Virginia when she and Winifred Nerney lunched with me in London, and I was given a brief description—in fact it consisted of one word—of what life had been like for a child and young girl in Dorothy's care. By that time Virginia was happily married, as she still is, to a Frenchman, and living in the North of France. She remained in contact with her former nurse, as with Winifred, who both loved her dearly. She has not seen the present book; but she has encouraged me to write it, and has welcomed its dedication to herself. I hope the result will not give her lasting distress. My aim has been, not to act as a Judge, but to tell the story of a friendship that lasted for twenty years.

It was one of the best of my very remarkable friendships with both men and women. If Bennett and I, in spite of the seventeen years' difference in our ages, of which at one time he admitted his incredulity, ever disagreed it was with amusement.

Marguerite, in one of her writings, described me as Bennett's 'disciple'. I was never anybody's disciple: however poor my work may be, it has always come from my own mind and imagination. When I once told Bennett how my mother and I had been alone in the house when I was born, he commented 'That explains a lot about you'—meaning that my obstinate independence, which he linked with self-help, even in the hour of birth, was accounted for. If he really did find me obstinate, he never said so, and I hope I was never tiresome to him. It was his nature to be patient and to treat all other people, from friends to children and waiters, as his equals.

To resume the narrative, after this lapse into egotism, I must report that Dorothy abandoned New York and returned to London in 1953. The last time I saw her was at a dinner given by the Society of Authors to celebrate the centenary of Bennett's birth. She arrived using a walking-stick which she jovially described as 'my third leg', and she attentively listened to all the speakers, who included A. P. Herbert, Margaret Drabble, Cecil Roberts, and myself. She herself did not speak. Until recently, whenever I wrote anything about Bennett, as I have always, from loyalty to his memory, done when invited, she made a point of sending me a commendatory letter; but I do not think she was unaware of my disapproval of much that she had done, and also my doubts about the authenticity of *A Portrait Done at Home.*

For a time her circumstances must have been far from easy. Fortunately, however, the value of Bennett's copyrights increased as his reputation passed into the history of English literature. With Marguerite's death she lost a rival claimant to their meagre earnings. She discovered a missing volume of the *Journal*, which was published as a Penguin; and she lived by herself, tended by a single maid, and latterly by a nurse, in a London flat. Strength remained with her until almost the end of her life.

She became, I am sure, more and more of a 'character' in old age, seeing very few people, but remaining her old autocratic self. She was tended with great kindness by the nurse, Nancy O'Flaherty, who, when illness became intense and Dorothy refused even to walk, found her a good nursing home where she could be given constant attention. Within forty-eight hours the Matron at the nursing home asked that she should be removed.

A hospital in Tooting Bec was then her refuge; and she stayed there for about a fortnight. Her condition became so serious, however, that she was put for the night under an oxygen tent; and next morning, when she seemed better, and was discussing with the nurse what she would have for breakfast, she suddenly fell back, dead. She was eighty-six, and had survived Bennett by nearly forty-six years.

She was duly cremated, in the presence of Virginia, Virginia's husband, a Cheston nephew, two business representatives, and a stranger who had long been an ardent admirer of Arnold Bennett's work. Her death was briefly reported in *The Times* and *The Daily Telegraph*; and the world has since heard nothing of her. She was a remarkable woman, whom Bennett unquestionably loved; but among his friends she had none who wished, once he was dead, to continue the acquaintance. I hope I have made it clear that, with myself, she showed none of her bad characteristics except restlessness, copiousness, and a wish to dabble in stocks and shares which might have ruined us both and left Virginia penniless.

It will have been observed that I have made no attempt to write Bennett's biography. This has been done in detail by others, most of whom never knew him. Nor have I tried to estimate the quality of his best and most enduring work. Now that I am old, I do not criticize. I read only favourite books; and 'let the lave go by me'. For this reason I am not competent to analyse what Bennett wrote. He took endless trouble over the details of every one of his books, trouble evidenced in a number of small notebooks and pocket diaries written in a hand so microscopic that I can no longer read it. Whether the novel is *Clayhanger* or *Riceyman Steps* it is the same; names, shops, street names, and what he called the 'ideas' so often sought for and discovered before he embarked on and during, the work of writing them by hand, often in a beautiful script, he was ever methodical. This was all part of his 'organization'.

He did not insist upon praise from his friends. Although he gave my wife inscribed copies of his later books, he gave me only one, *Paris Nights*, and I think his other friends had the same experience. That is to say, he would not embarrass them by seeming to invite praise. Nor would he accept dedications. Modesty was the keynote of his nature. On the publication of *The Roll Call* I made some strictures on that book, to which he replied 'What you say confirms my belief that I can only write well about characters I knew before I was twenty-one.'

On the whole that is the view of readers who miss the scrupulous integrity of such work as one of his best, *Lord Raingo*. Time will decide; and even Shakespeare was not always at his best and most serious.

Now I am done. I hope what I have written will not be thought an exercise in self-display. My sole object has been to present the man I knew; a man who has been more written about, often with animus and misjudgment, than any of his contemporaries.

APPENDIX

FRANK SWINNERTON
by ARNOLD BENNETT

(written in 1917 as part of the Publicity on the American edition of Nocturne, *published by George H. Doran, for which edition H. G. Wells wrote an Introduction. Such sponsorship led to the book's success in the United States)*

There was nothing in the slightest degree romantic or marvellous in my first meeting with Frank Swinnerton. It all happened in the most ordinary way. One day, perhaps eight or nine years ago, I received a novel entitled *The Young Idea.* I was then living in a very mediaeval *pavilion* in an old quarter of Paris. I remember quite well that an American friend came for Christmas Eve dinner in this fastness or fortress. I had a new and wondrous coffee-machine of which I was proud, and in which I made the coffee with my own hands. On that night I put the ground coffee in the wrong end of the machine, with the result that finally the precious liquid inundated the whole of the sideboard instead of reaching the cups; also the mediaeval oil-lamps were left with the wicks too high in the drawing-room, so that when we returned to the drawing-room after mopping up the coffee, every object therein was evenly covered with a coat of greasy black soot, and the opaque atmosphere scorched the eyes and parched the throat.

To return to *The Young Idea.* The book was accompanied by a short, rather curt note from the author, Frank Swinnerton, politely indicating that if I cared to read it he would be glad, and implying that if I didn't care to read it, he should endeavour still to survive. I would quote the letter, but I cannot find it—no doubt for the reason that all my correspondence is carefully filed on the most modern filing system. I did not read *The Young Idea* for a long time. Why should I consecrate three irrecoverable hours or so to the work of a man as to whom I had no credentials? Why should I thus introduce foreign matter into the delicate cogwheels of my programme of reading? However, after a delay of weeks, heaven in its deep wisdom inspired me with a caprice to pick up the volume.

I had read, without fatigue but on the other hand without passionate eagerness, about a hundred pages before the thought suddenly occurred to me: 'I do not remember having yet come across one single ready-made phrase in this story.' Such was my first definable thought concerning Frank Swinnerton. I hate ready-made phrases, which in my view—and in that of Schopenhauer—are the sure mark of a mediocre writer. I began to be interested. I soon said to myself: 'This fellow has a distinguished style.' I then perceived that the character-drawing was both subtle and original, the atmosphere delicious, and the movement of the tale very original, too. The novel stirred me—not by its powerfulness, for it did not set out to be powerful—but by its individuality and distinction. I thereupon wrote to Frank Swinnerton. I forget entirely what I said. But I know that I decided that I must meet him.

When I came to London, considerably later, I took measures to meet him, at the Authors' Club. He proved to be young; I daresay twenty-four or twenty-five—medium height, medium looks, medium clothes, somewhat reddish hair, and lively eyes. If I had seen him in a motorbus I should never have said: 'A remarkable chap,'—no more than if I had seen myself in a motorbus. My impressions of the interview were rather like my impressions of the book; at first somewhat negative, and only very slowly becoming positive. He was reserved, as became a young author; I was reserved, as became an older author; we were both reserved, as became Englishmen. Our views on the most important thing in the world—that is to say, fiction—agreed, not completely, but in the main; it would never have done for us to agree completely. I was as much pleased by what he didn't say as by what he said; quite as much by the indications of the stock inside the shop as by the display in the window. The interview came to a calm close. My knowledge of him acquired from it amounted to this, that he held decided and righteous views upon literature, that his heart was not on his sleeve, and that he worked in a publisher's office during the day and wrote for himself in the evenings.

Then I saw no more of Swinnerton for a relatively long period. I read other books of his. I read *The Casement*, and *The Happy Family*, and, I think, his critical work on George Gissing. *The Happy Family* marked a new stage in his development. It has some really piquant scenes, and it revealed that minute knowledge of middle-class life in the nearer suburbs of London, and that disturbing insight into the hearts and brains of quite unfashionable girls, which are two of his principal gifts. I read a sketch of his of a commonplace crowd walking round a bandstand which brought me to a real decision as to his qualities. The thing was like life, and it was bathed in poetry.

Our acquaintance proceeded slowly, and I must be allowed to assert that the initiative which pushed it forward was mine. It made a jump when he spent a week-end in the Thames Estuary on my yacht. If any reader has a curiosity to know what my yacht is not like, he should read the striking yacht chapter in *Nocturne*. I am convinced that Swinnerton evolved the yacht in *Nocturne* from my yacht; but he ennobled, magnified, decorated, enriched and bejewelled it till honestly I could not recognize my wretched vessel. The yacht in *Nocturne* is the yacht I want, ought to have, and never shall have. I envy him the yacht in *Nocturne*, and my envy takes a malicious pleasure in pointing out a mistake in the glowing scene. He anchors his yacht in the middle of the Thames—as if the tyrannic authorities of the Port of London would ever allow a yacht, or any other craft, to anchor in midstream!

After the brief cruise our friendship grew rapidly. I now know Swinnerton—probably as well as any man knows him; I have penetrated into the interior of the shop. He has done several things since I first knew him—rounded the corner of thirty, grown a beard, under the orders of a doctor, and physically matured. Indeed he looks decidedly stronger than in fact he is—he was never able to pass the medical examination for the army. He is still in the business of publishing, being one of the principal personages in the ancient and well-tried firm of Chatto and Windus, the English publishers of Swinburne and Mark Twain. He reads manuscripts, including his own—and including mine. He refuses manuscripts, though he did accept one of mine. He tells authors what they ought to do and ought not to do. He is marvellously and terribly particular and fussy about the format of the books issued by his firm. Questions as to founts of type, width of margins, disposition of title-pages, tint and texture of bindings really do interest him. And misprints—especially when he has read the proofs himself—give him neuralgia and even worse afflictions. Indeed he is the ideal publisher for an author.

Nevertheless, publishing is only a side-line of his. He still writes for himself in the evenings and at week-ends—the office never sees him on Saturdays. Among the chief literary events of nineteen seventeen was *Nocturne*, which he wrote in the evenings and at week-ends. It is a short book, but the time in which he wrote it was even shorter. He had scarcely begun it when it was finished. In regard to the result I am prepared to say to the judicious reader unacquainted with Swinnerton's work, 'Read *Nocturne*',—and to stand or fall, and to let him stand or fall, by the result. *Nocturne* moved H. G. Wells to an extraordinary enthusiasm, so much so that Wells had to write to the morning papers about it. And I remember Wells saying to me: 'You know, Arnold, he achieves a perfection in *Nocturne* that you and I never get within streets of.' A hard saying to pass between two hardened pilgrims whose combined years total over a century; but justified. You can say what you like about *Nocturne*, but you cannot say that on its own scale it is not perfect, consummate. At least, I cannot.

Besides being no mean publisher and a novelist who has produced several fine and one perfect novel, Frank Swinnerton has other gifts. He is a surpassingly good raconteur. By which I do not signify that the man who meets Swinnerton for the first, second or third time will infallibly ache with laughter at his remarks. Swinnerton only blossoms in the right atmosphere; he must know exactly where he is; he must be perfectly sure of his environment, before the flower uncloses. And he merely relates what he has seen, what he has taken part in. The narrations would be naught if he were not the narrator. His effects are helped by the fact that he is an excellent mimic and by his utter realistic mercilessness. But like all first-class realists he is also a romantic, and in his mercilessness there is a mysterious touch of fundamental benevolence—as befits the attitude of one who does not worry because human nature is not something different from what it actually is. Lastly, in this connection, he has superlatively the laugh known as the 'infectious laugh'. When he laughs everybody laughs, everybody has to laugh. There are men who tell side-splitting tales with the face of an undertaker—for example, Irvin Cobb. There are men who tell side-splitting tales and openly and candidly rollick in them from the first word; and of these latter is Frank Swinnerton. But Frank Swinnerton can be more cruel than Irvin Cobb. Indeed, sometimes, when he is telling a story, his face becomes exactly like the face of Mephistopheles in excellent humour with the world's sinfulness and idiocy.

Swinnerton's other gift is the critical. It has been said that an author cannot be at once a first-class critic and a first-class creative artist. To which absurdity I reply: What about William Dean Howells? And what about Henry James, to name no other names? Anyhow, if Swinnerton excels in fiction he also excels in literary criticism. The fact that the literary editor of *The Manchester Guardian* wrote and asked him to write literary criticism for *The Manchester Guardian* will perhaps convey nothing to the American citizen. But to the Englishman of literary taste and experience it has enormous import. *The Manchester Guardian* publishes the most fastidious and judicious literary criticism in Britain.

I recall that once when Swinnerton was in my house I had there also a young military officer with a mad passion for letters and a terrific ambition to be an author. The officer gave me a manuscript to read. I handed it over to Swinnerton to read, and then called upon Swinnerton to criticize it in the presence of both of us. 'Your friend is very kind,' said the officer to me afterwards, 'but it was a frightful ordeal.'

The book on George Gissing I have already mentioned. But it was Swinnerton's work on R. L. Stevenson that made the trouble in London. It is a destructive work. It is very bland and impartial, and not bereft of laudatory passages, but since its appearance Stevenson's reputation has never been the same. Those who wish to preserve their illusions about the greatness of Stevenson should refrain from reading it. Few recent books of criticism have aroused more hostility than Swinnerton's *Stevenson*. There is a powerful Stevenson cult in England, as there is in America. And in London there are sundry persons who cannot get far into any conversation without using the phrase, 'As dear old R.L.S. used to say.' Some of these persons are personages. They rage at the mention of Swinnerton. One of them on a celebrated occasion exclaimed in fury: 'Never let me hear that man's name!' This detail alone shows that Swinnerton is a real critic. Sham criticism, however violent,—and Swinnerton is incapable of violence—does not and cannot arouse such passion.

INDEX